Sermons for Special Occasions

Brendan Hoban

In memory of my mother,
Ellen Hoban 1914-1999,
a prophet in her own country.

CONTENTS

Foreword

TO preach to priests on preaching, someone said, you have to be either very learned or very holy. *Foolish* is another word that comes to mind and *pretentious* and *arrogant* are floating around there somewhere too. So inevitably these offerings are presented in a tentative if not apologetic way.

Yet the fact is that apart from the occasional very gifted speaker, most priests preach on a Sunday morning not because they feel passionately they have something to say but because they sense a duty to say something. And we need all the help we can get. Those of us who face a white sheet of paper on a Saturday morning (yes, I know the theory is that you start on Monday morning) and, particularly, those of us who have been around the track of the three-year cycle more times than we care to remember, often find ourselves looking for some bit of inspiration, some new approach, some different line that might help to get started. Or lighten the load.

And load it is. The Sunday sermon is a bit like a load in a wheelbarrow - it seems to be forever there in front of us - and the people in the seats generally have little idea of how hassled priests get over sermons. For instance, few people realise the relief with which priests often receive a pastoral letter from the bishop with instructions that it be read out - not because of the wisdom it contains or the new ground it breaks but - because it relieves us of having to prepare a sermon for that weekend. No wonder Sisyphus of Corinth is a kind of patron saint of preachers. He was the unfortunate who was condemned forever to push the rock to the top of the hill and watch it roll down again to the bottom. Preparing sermons feels a bit like that, for most of us, much of the time.

9

Our instinct is right. Sermons are difficult. Writing for talking is an uncommon skill. Eliciting the question in the mind of the hearers that the gospel truth will address is no easy task. Searching interminably for a memorable phrase that can carry the thought into the rest of Sunday can ruin a Saturday. Our best efforts are often unfavourably compared with gifted communicators on radio and television. People demand more now from the struggling preacher. And there's no shortage of advice: keep it short, have an arresting opening and a clean ending, keep it interesting, make one point, use few quotations or statistics, repeat for the sake of clarity, pare it down, the importance of sequence, no extra time.

So we need all the help we can get. Especially with the growing number of unusual occasions when we are expected to put a few words together: the centenary of a school, a harvest Mass, jubilee of a church, death by suicide, graduation Mass, leaving a parish and so on. So this selection is offered in the knowledge that while every effective sermon we preach has to come from within ourselves, it can help to see how someone else gets a handle on things, if only to get started.

Brendan Hoban

CHRISTMAS NIGHT
Clearances

THERE'S a poem by Seamus Heaney called *Clearances*
written in memory of his mother. In it he remembers the
parish priest anointing his mother as she died. Around her
bedside were members of her family, some answering the
prayers, some crying. A scene from his childhood flashed into his
mind. It was a Sunday morning and the rest of the family were
at second Mass. His mother was peeling potatoes at the kitchen
sink and he was helping her, standing between her and the sink.
As they peeled the potatoes the skins fell one by one 'like solder
weeping off the soldering iron' and splashed into a bucket of clear
water. There was between mother and child a togetherness, an
understanding, a sympathy, a communion, a closeness that they
were never to recapture. 'I remembered her head bent towards
my head / Her breath in mine, our fluent dipping knives / Never
closer the whole rest of our lives'.

For some reason that poem always comes into my mind on
Christmas night. It's an echo of Seamus Heaney's childhood, it's
a memory evoked by an incident, an occasion, a point in life that
suddenly confronts us.

Death is like that and so too is Christmas. Because Christmas
is more than just something we celebrate at a particular time of
a particular year. Christmas, in a sense, always has echoes of the
Christmases of the past. Christmas is an occasion steeped in
faith and flesh and memory. It's peopled with those we love or
have loved, those whose presence we enjoy and those we now
miss. Christmas is about memories good and bad but never
indifferent. It's about people and places and things and it evokes
for each of us our own personal memory.

For me Christmas night is about watching my father and mother (God rest them) through the rails of a kitchen chair as we knelt to say the Rosary. It's hearing my father say, before we got up off our knees on Christmas night, 'Go mbeirmid beo ar an am seo arís' - a prayer that we all might be alive and well the following Christmas.

For me Christmas is about the early three Masses in a row on Christmas morning, the excitement or the disillusionment of Santa Claus, the turkey glowing in the oven, the plum pudding and the custard and the sweet cake, what were in simpler times, the exotic fare of Christmas day.

We can't help remembering at Christmas, because Christmas is about remembering, remembering not just the people or the places of its celebration but remembering too how it all started and what it's all about.

In a backward place, a very long time ago, a young woman pregnant with a baby who wasn't her husband's was refused admittance to an inn and she went into a stable where the cattle sheltered and there she gave birth to a baby boy, she wrapped him in swaddling clothes and laid him in a manger.

It was by all external accounts a shabby and pathetic little scene but for us 2000 years later it was the beginning of the greatest story ever told. It was the start of the greatest adventure that humankind has ever experienced because it contained within it the seed of human fulfilment and human happiness.

Into a world of conflict and war, Jesus the son of God brought a message of peace and reconciliation, into lives broken by selfishness and sin he brought the healing balm of acceptance and forgiveness. Into a way of life that was compromised by attitudes of fear and distrust and disharmony of all kinds he brought a message of faith and hope and love.

It's the message of the Crib. It's what we now call 'the mystery of the incarnation'. To make something 'incarnate' is to make it flesh, to make it real. And that's what happened. 'The Word was made flesh'. The Son, the Second person of the Trinity, was made flesh. God, in other words, became a human being. Jesus, the Son of God and the Son of Mary, is God translated into a language that we can understand. Jesus is God close to us.

Tonight we're remembering that occasion captured in the

simplicity of the Crib. God has entered into human history in the person of a baby on a bed of straw. What the Jews had longed for, what the Scriptures had foretold had come true. In a literal and extraordinary way because of the happening captured in the experience of the Crib, nothing could ever be the same again. God had entered into human history and everything was changed and changed utterly.

And that's why Christmas is above all a time for celebration. It's because of what the Crib means and what it begun that as Christian people our hearts should burst with joy and celebration. That at least is what should happen at Christmastime. But we know too that in a world where so many of us just live and partly live, the strains and difficulties of human existence can temper our Christian celebration.

Christmas is a strange time because it surfaces who and what we are. It reminds us about what we have and what we haven't. Christmas is like a clearance in the forest when we can't see the wood from the trees. Christmas creates a space that gives us a chance to look at our lives again.

Nuala O'Faolain, in her book, *Are you Somebody?* paints a picture of the desolation of her Christmas, the experience of going away on her own to a place in Clare, walking the Burren on Christmas Day, having a meal on her own, meeting nobody. Paul Durcan has a poem about Christmas in which he writes about spending St Stephen's Day watching a phone that never rings. Christmas, he writes, is 'the Feast of St Loneliness.' You can feel the pain between the paragraphs of Nuala O'Faolain's book. You can read the pain between the lines of Paul Durcan's poem because Christmas has a way of surfacing what we don't want to face for the rest of the year.

Christmas opens old wounds; it stirs memories we want to keep buried; it forces a kind of life's stock-taking on us; it welcomes the demons that we want to keep safely buried beneath the surface of our lives.

This Christmas time somewhere in Ireland a separated father will take his young children to Supermacs on the day after Christmas Day and he'll watch the clock in Supermacs until it's time for him to take them back to their mother. And they'll cry when he has to go as they do every St Stephen's Day. They'll cry because they won't want him to go and something deep inside

13

himself will tell him that he doesn't want to go either, but go he will because, for whatever way the cards of his life have fallen, go, he feels, he must. And variations on that scene will be replayed over and over again in thousands of Irish homes this Christmas.

For some people this will be the happiest Christmas of their lives, the first Christmas they'll spend in their new home or with their new baby or maybe just together. For others it will be an unhappy Christmas filled with memories of a loved one who died during the course of the year. For some Christmas will mean welcoming home brothers and sisters and sons and daughters from Dublin and England and far away. For others it will mean remembering those brothers and sisters and sons and daughters who for one reason or another can't be home this Christmas.

For some families, it'll mean the excitement of Santa Claus and for other people Christmas is the loneliest time of the year. But whatever our Christmas will be, whatever it is that God has laid out for us, let us remember that behind it all is the presence among us of someone who came into our hostile world as a fragile baby. Someone who came so that we might have life and live it to the full. Someone who came to bring a message of joy and of love and of peace. Someone who came to tell us how we should live and the kind of people we should be, and above all Someone who became a member of my family and yours.

So, on this holiest of nights, we think of those who have come home and we welcome them. We think of our relatives and friends who are far away from home and we pray for them. We think of our loved ones who have died during the year and despite the sadness and the loss and the pain we try to rejoice in the happiness that God has given them. We think of the poor whom Jesus loved especially and of our obligations to them. We think of the sins we have committed and our sorrow for them. We think of the God who took our flesh and became one of us, and how we should thank him for it.

Glory to God in the highest and peace on earth to those who are his friends. On this holy night, in your name, I give him glory. In his name, I wish you peace. On this holiest of nights may God be with you and your families wherever they may be.

14

WEDDING ANNIVERSARY
A golden thanksgiving

THIS occasion speaks for itself. So it would be inappropriate to give a long sermon on marriage or even on values like faithfulness or perseverance or happiness or solidarity or respect or love that are so much part of the atmosphere of this occasion. And I know that John and Mary wouldn't thank me if I started praising them or talking about them for a long time.

At the same time I feel that this occasion shouldn't pass without saying a few words about what it all means.

First, on behalf of all who have gathered here, a word of congratulations to them on fifty years of married life. Half a century, five decades is a fair slice of life. Even though the years have a way of slipping by quietly and quickly, fifty years is a long time. Few couples live to see it together so let us on this day give praise and thanks to God for the years they have spent together and for the gifts that God has given them all these years.

Looking back today on their fifty years together, I'm sure that it holds many happy memories for them: the day of their wedding, the birth of their children, the birth of their grandchildren. And I'm sure too that they had their share of sorrows. Life for everyone is a great mix of things, good days and bad days, times of great happiness and times of great sadness, the joyful mysteries and the sorrowful mysteries of the last fifty years are now part of a great memory bank that will remain with them all their days.

The world that John and Mary were married in fifty years ago was very different from the world we live in today. We complain a lot nowadays about how difficult life is and how stressed out and busy people often are. And about the poverty and deprivation that still lingers on despite the prosperity of recent years. And all of that is true. But work and poverty are nothing like they were. They don't compare with the poverty and deprivation and the drudgery of fifty years ago.

We often hear people say now how difficult it is to rear children in today's world. But it was never easy. Particularly at a time when work was scarce, when the resources we take for granted now like piped water, electricity and so on were no more than a dream, when second-level education was available only to the privileged few, when emigration and the loneliness that attended it weren't choices that were made but inevitable realities of economic life.

So John and Mary can be proud and happy of the harvest of the last fifty years: the children they reared, the work they did, the contribution they made to the life of townland and parish. They can indeed be proud of their eight children who have organised this celebration for them today and happy too that their children recognise that their parents' faith in God and the things of God are so special to them that they would want this celebration to begin with Mass.

John and Mary, this Mass and later on the celebration in the hotel are a tribute to the respect and love and, above all, the appreciation that your children and grandchildren have for you. They appreciate you both as the people you are, loved and loving parents, and the unrepayable contribution you have made to their lives in everything you have given to your children: life itself, the nurturing that brought them through the early years, the support that you always gave them and not least the faith that remains so much part of your life and so much part of theirs.

Your children know that what they have received from you is unquantifiable. They know that, no matter what they do for as long as you are with them on this earth, they will never be able to repay the contribution that they received from you in the early, impressionable and vital years in your home in Carrowpadden. All they can do, through a symbolic occasion like this, is let *you* know that *they* know how much it all means to them. All they can do is let you know that the love and the care and the support and the nurturing that they received from you is acknowledged and appreciated and marked on this happy, golden day.

The word *Eucharist* means thanksgiving and this Mass is above all a prayer of thanksgiving for the long and happy married life that you have had together over the last fifty years; for the children you brought into the world and for their children in turn; for all your neighbours and friends who accompanied you on your journey through life; for all the bits and pieces that go to make up the memory bank of the last half century.

And this Mass too is an opportunity to ask God to bless you both with continued health and happiness in the years to come.

On this special occasion, as we gather to celebrate fifty golden years of marriage and of family, may you have everything your family would wish you to have on this day.

HARVEST THANKSGIVING

What earth has given, what hands have made

NO matter how old or young we may be, in all of our lives there are particular moments when we learned something special. I don't mean the high points of our lives like when people get married or children are born or that kind of thing. What I mean is that, on some ordinary day in some ordinary place, we suddenly realise something that's desperately important. We get some insight into life and we know instinctively that we'll never forget it.

I remember on one occasion watching a football match on television in the company of a man who was blind. He was a great football fan, he had played football in his youth, and he had lost his sight but not his great interest in football. I remember that occasion graphically. As we watched everything that happened in Croke Park – every score, every bounce of the ball – he listened to the commentary.

I knew at the time that I would never forget that experience because for the first time in my life I appreciated to some degree at least what it must mean to be blind and how precious the gift of sight is. And I remember at the time feeling very guilty that at no time in my life had I ever thanked God for the gift of sight.

Of course we do that all the time. We take for granted so many of the precious gifts of God. We fill our minds with all that is wrong with the world and with our world and we forget about all the things that are right about it. We complain because we haven't all the things that we think we need and we forget about all the things that we have.

We sing what's probably the most popular song in the world, the *If Only* song - if only I won the Lotto, if only I lived in a different place or had different parents or different children or a different job. How many of us spend our lives looking at the green fields far away and we're not able to feel the grass growing under our feet? How many of us live lives full of unrealistic expectations and we're not able to count the blessings that God has showered on us? It is, for many, a fact of life that we find it difficult to appreciate the value of what we take so much for granted.

So today, even just for today, let's try to forget about the *Ifs* and *Buts* of life and let's thank God for the many and varied gifts he has given us - the health of mind and body that are so precious, the children growing up in our parish, the jobs so many are so lucky to have, the work that people do, the fresh air that we breathe every day, the friendship and loyalty that we experience so often, the love of parents and children and husbands and wives for each other, the faith that is so obvious in so many people's lives.

That's not to say that appreciating what we have means ignoring the darker side of life. Today the sun will rise on a world where life is sometimes not that precious, where thousands of people will go to bed hungry, on homes where children are abused, where wives are beaten, where spouses take each other for granted, where parents don't live up to their responsibilities, where the poor are ignored, where the homeless are moved on or shut out, where the lonely are neglected - and all of that is true, some of it far from home, some of it very close to home.

But today too the sun will rise on children who are cherished, on spouses who love each other, on houses with cupboards and fridges filled with food, on homes full of warmth and kindness and love. Today the sun will rise on these and on a thousand gifts of God that we take so much for granted.

So today, in this Harvest Mass of Thanksgiving, we are simply saying thanks to God for the many gifts and blessings of the past year. What we are saying really is that God is the source of all life, that everything that exists, everything that grows, everything there is finds its roots in a world that God created.

What we mean too is that everything that exists, everything that grows, everything there is, is kept in existence by a God who loved us into life and a God who sustains everything we have and everything we are. And every time we take bread and wine and offer them to God in the Eucharist, every time we do that we offer all of life and everything there is and everything we are to the God in whose image each of us is made and the God who sustains the life each one of us enjoys.

And especially today as we celebrate our Harvest Mass of Thanksgiving, when we offer the bread and wine of this Mass we are offering the work and the produce of the work, the gifts that have come our way that are the fruits of God's earth and the work of our hands. And the produce and the items that are here around the altar represent the work and the labour of the last year.

So what we are doing today is above all giving thanks to God for the circle of growing and reaping that nature follows so regularly. Giving thanks for the produce of our fields, for the harvest reaped from the sea, for the fruits of life and career and family. Giving thanks for the work that was done in the home, in business, on the farm or at sea. Giving thanks for the money that was earned and for the health of life and body that made it all possible. What we are saying today is that everything is a gift from God and depending on how we use those gifts, life can be enhanced or diminished.

So today as we offer up these symbols of God's care and love for us, we offer them with their joyful mysteries and their sorrowful mysteries. We thank God for the life and the love and the joy they have given. We ask his forgiveness for any harm we may have done through them. All of these gifts are summed up in the offering of the bread in the words 'Blessed are you, Lord God of all creation, through *your* goodness *we* have this bread to offer which earth has given and human hands have made, it will become for us, the bread of life.' The bread and wine are the symbols that tell us that everything there is begins and ends with God.

LIMBO AND THE UNBAPTISED

Grieving our dead children

I remember, many years ago giving a sermon about baptism and mentioning in passing that there was no such place as Limbo. After Mass an old woman came into the sacristy. She was in her Eighties and, with tears streaming down her face, she told me how happy she was at what I'd just said about Limbo.

She told me her story. She had had several miscarriages and her babies were buried in a field behind the house and every morning, when she got out of bed, she went to the window and she looked out over the field and she prayed that her babies would one day be happy with God. My words, confused and unintentional though they were, had suddenly lifted a great weight from her shoulders.

It was a great learning experience for me because for the first time in my life I got some insight into the pain involved for parents who lose a baby in the womb or shortly after birth. And, in particular, the anguish of such parents in the past when unbaptised babies were said to be separated from God and so could not be buried in 'consecrated' ground.

I got some *insight* but not *understanding* because to understand, to really understand that loss, that pain, you have to go through it. And it's only those who experience it, it's only those who walk that road who know what it means.

So we need to establish very clearly in our minds that important truth: that all of our children who died in the womb or after birth, all of our children baptised or unbaptised are now enjoying the happiness of heaven.

There was a time, as we all know, when it was said that if a child died without baptism that child was separated from God, that child was in Limbo. I want to say two things very clearly about that: one is that there never was a place called Limbo, that there never was, for our unbaptised children, any question of them being separated from God. And the second thing I want to do is to apologise, on behalf of our Church, for the pain and the hurt that Limbo caused to God knows how many generations of parents.

It was wrong; it caused unimaginable hurt; it diminished and warped our image of a loving God; and, on behalf of all who were hurt by that teaching and by the refusal to allow unbaptised children to be buried in consecrated ground, which was based on that teaching, I apologise and ask forgiveness for the wrong our church has done.

I know that words are cheap; I know that nothing can undo that injustice; I know that there is nothing we can do to lessen that river of pain and hurt that enveloped and damaged so many. But at the same time we can at least say that we know something of the terrible pain that is the legacy of that teaching and we can at least put on public record the hurt we have caused as a Church.

Maybe too there is something we can do at a local or a parish level to record in some way that hurt and pain and to hold in memory those precious, precious children who are now happy with God.

Some parishes have built a permanent monument to the memory of these children. Others have set in place a stained-glass window with an appropriate design. Others have a book of Remembrance listing all the children's names and retain it in a place of honour in the church.

Others again, as families, have claimed and named these children as their own. Including children who died in the womb. Some people may feel this is a bit extreme, and to tell you the truth, that's what I once thought myself. But not now.

When I was growing up, there were six of us in the family, six children. Then I learnt one day in passing that my mother had given birth to triplets, 2 girls and a boy, two sisters and a brother I never knew I had. I didn't pay much attention to it; my mother never mentioned it; it was never referred to or discussed. That was the way it was.

Then a week or so before my mother died, a nurse in

Castlebar hospital coming on duty asked her who she was, and my mother told the nurse her name and then she said immediately to the nurse: "I had triplets in this hospital over fifty years ago."

What a shock it was to realise that all of fifty-six years later my mother still grieved her three dead children. Some months after she died, we got the death certificates in Castlebar. We found out that the children were born prematurely: one girl lived a quarter of an hour, the boy lived one day and the other girl lived two days, and after we got the certificates we decided as a family to name them Anthony, Ann and Catherine. All I can say is that it was important for us to name and to claim them as our own.

I mention this because I feel there may be others, who may be helped if they name their sons or daughters or brothers and sisters and if they claim them as part of their families.

I know that may be too painful for some people and the last thing I would want to do would be to surface a pain that people aren't able to bear. But I know too that reflecting however gently on the sadness associated with what is for many individuals and families a dark and difficult area can bring healing and consolation.

We owe that much to the children whose lives may have been short but whose memory is precious. And we owe it to ourselves to own their lives and to hold them in memory.

INTER-CHURCH WEDDING
The greatest of these

*S*O *faith, hope and love, these three and the greatest of them is love (1 Cor. Chapter13:13)*
What we are doing here today is celebrating the love that has led Mary and John through the detours of these last years to this place on this day.

Love, as we all know, is a two-sided coin. It has its joyful mysteries and its sorrowful mysteries. But today is a day for celebrating, a day for rejoicing because today John and Mary are giving their love a decisive expression in this public commitment that we call 'marriage', a public commitment that goes far beyond this particular public, or this particular place. A public commitment in love that asks God to be their witness.

And this public commitment takes place in this church, in Mary's church (as it happens) in this place that holds special memories for her as she grew up in this faith-community. This building represents a place steeped in the values and the traditions that have over the centuries given substance to the content and the practice of our Christian faith.

Here the Christian story has been told and retold, here people have gathered for worship, couples have been married, babies baptised, the dead buried.

So for Mary this church is a place that sings a silent hymn to the things that in life and in death mean most to us.

This is a place where we come to worship our God, this is a place where we take time out, to pray, to reflect, to pick over the bits and pieces of our lives, and to place in God's hands the hopes and the dreams, the worries and difficulties that are part and parcel of every life.

And today Mary has invited John to this special place to exchange their marriage vows. John comes from a different religious tradition, and he brings with him everything that he is as a person, and formed by the faith of his religious tradition, he brings with him everything that makes him what he is today.

We welcome John today not just as an individual person who just happens to be getting married in our church, we welcome him acknowledging the richness of the Christian faith that he brings from his own tradition.

And as John and Mary come together in this place and at this time, part of the richness of this gathering, is not just the love that they have for each other, or the joy that is part of this occasion but the respect which they bring to the different faith traditions from which they come. And just as the love they have for each other will enrich each other's lives in the future, so too their different faith traditions will enrich their individual faith lives in the future.

So they have come to make a public expression before each other, before their families, before their friends and before their God, to make a public expression of their love for each other and of a permanent commitment that they undertake to sustain that love into the future.

And this place is, if you like, a kind of intersection, a meeting-place, a crossroads, where the pilgrimage that is their journey of love, and their journey of faith finds substance and direction.

I like that notion of journey. It has in it a dynamic of change and a dynamic of non-change. On a journey, everything changes and yet in a peculiar way everything remains the same. And there's a sense in which life itself is that kind of journey. There's a sense that from birth to death each of us travels the great journey of life. And from time to time along that road of life things happen to us and we make things happen to us that change our lives significantly..

There are (as we all know) great parts of life, great chunks of that journey that we can't control. But we know too that there are parts of life that we can control, that we can change for better or for worse.

There are crossroads that we meet in life that are there whether we like it or not and there are crossroads that we shape for ourselves because of the choices we make in life.

Today Mary and John have created a crossroads for themselves, a crossroads that is very much of their own making. They were both brought up in different places, in different families, in different faith-traditions and somewhere along the road of life their paths crossed. There was an intersection that was to change their lives completely, that was to align in unexpected ways the two journeys they were on.

It could have been just another meeting between two people but from that point on, their lives and their future started to come together. That happened because they decided it should happen and today they are making another decision that confirms their intention to travel forever along whatever road of life awaits them from this point in time.

In the years since they've met their love for each other has grown to such a degree that they have decided before families, before friends and before God, they have decided in this public and formal way to be married as a Christian couple.

The intersection of their lives that took place when they met wasn't just an intersection between two people. It was between two people brought up in two different religious traditions. It was the intersection to some degree of two faith communities. And while there is much that Mary and John share as faith-people, while there is much that each can identify with in the other's faith, they know too that there are differences of emphasis and of belief that they do not share. And that is part not just of the reality of this day but part of the richness of what is now, for them, a shared pilgrimage.

But in terms specifically of what's happening here today their faith intersects and resonates completely. Because their belief in Christian marriage is a shared belief, a shared belief in a commitment to faithfulness and fidelity to one another, a shared belief in a commitment to the permanency of their marriage, a shared belief in a commitment to a shared life where fidelity and permanency will create an atmosphere of acceptance, of trust and of love that will help them to overcome the tensions and the failures that are part and parcel of every human relationship.

Mary and John both believe that Christian marriage is about sharing, a sharing that is complete and absolute, a sharing of hearts and bodies and minds, a sharing of time, of decisions, of material possessions, a sharing of ideas, of feelings, of attitudes, as complete a sharing as it is possible to have. And they know too that Christian marriage is above all a sharing of love.

It's a statement that the love that has brought them to this day will be made to grow and to deepen all the days of their lives.

It's a commitment they will make that from now on they will mingle their two lives into one, together and forever; they will live and love and grow, together and forever; they will live a community of love, together and forever.

For John and Mary, today is for them the end of one dream and the beginning of another. It's our prayer for them today that that their dream will come true.

Our prayer for them is that as they face the future together that their lives may be full of kindness, of understanding and of forgiveness.

Life (as we all know) is full of ups and downs, good times and bad times, joys and sorrows.

May the love that they share today and the support that God gives them in their married life help them to grow closer through the ups and downs of life.

SUICIDE
Do not let your hearts be troubled

O N Good Friday, we remember the crucifixion of our Lord
and Saviour Jesus Christ on Calvary. On Holy Saturday
night we celebrate his resurrection. These two great events –
crucifixion and resurrection – are high points in the history of
our faith.

Jesus died on Calvary and in his dying he redeemed us from
our sins and in his resurrection, in his triumph over death, he
pointed the way for those of us who believe in him as our Lord
and Saviour.

We gather this morning for this funeral Mass for PJ. On
behalf of all who have gathered here, I offer our sympathy and
support to his father, brother, sisters, relatives and friends and
not least to his neighbours and friends who were a very special
part of his life.

We gather during Holy Week so we gather in the context of
crucifixion and resurrection to celebrate the Christian rituals of
death and burial. PJ believed in what the crucifixion and the
resurrection represented and strengthened by that faith, we
gather to offer the joyful mysteries and the sorrowful mysteries
of his life to the God who loved him in life and now welcomes
him in death.

These Easter days are dominated by crucifixion and
resurrection and it is in that context that we come to celebrate
PJ's life, to pray for the happy repose of his soul and to ask God
to bring him into the peace and contentment of his heavenly
home.

Some time ago I listened to a theologian talking about life,
talking about the way we cope with life, talking about what

meaning it has and what meaning it sometimes hasn't. He talked too about the times in life when we're broken and the times when, despite our faith, we begin to wonder what life is all about. And he talked about the need at such times to confront the areas of meaninglessness in our lives. The need for us to face the fact that at times and on occasions God can seem far away from us. And at such times and on such occasions the need to support one another through that experience of meaninglessness.

I can't speak for everyone here, but I sense something of that restlessness in us now. Something a bit beyond the ordinary restlessness that we learn to accept, and more often than not, to some degree at least learn to control. And that's not unusual when death comes.

PJ is dead and his death brings with it the sense of loss and regret and sadness that death often carries in its wake. We find inevitably that death disturbs us, that it sets us at odds with ourselves. It disturbs the easy pattern of our lives; it disrupts the usual parameters within which our existence in this world is shaped; it sets aside the boundaries that ordinarily reassure us and we are left floundering in the great mystery of it all.

Last week we went to the shops or we collected the children from school or we did the one thousand and one ordinary everyday things that make up the lives we lead. And then suddenly we find ourselves at a funeral of a loved one and in the space of a week or a few days or even a few hours our lives are turned upside down.

Even though we're used to funerals, even though people die every day of the week, even though we take death and dying for granted, the death of someone we love is a difficult and traumatic experience. Death, someone said, is usually like the sound of a gentle flute which we hear complaining in the distance but the death of a loved one is like a brass band playing in our front garden.

So even though we sense that restlessness, even though we find ourselves out of sync with life, the first thing we have to do is to remind ourselves, difficult though it may be in the welter of emotions that come and go so quickly, that this is what death does to those who mourn their loved ones.

This experience of loss and regret and sadness, this experience of being at odds with ourselves is what grieving a death is. And there are questions as there always are with the death of a loved one - questions that jump out at us in every waking hour, questions that lie in wait for us and that tumble out of our minds at the most unexpected moment, regrets that we haunt ourselves with, the litany of *If onlys* that make us want to play back the tape of PJ's life and death so that we could write a different script for him.

But that's outside and beyond what's within our power to make happen. Instead what we have to do this Holy Week, when we remember the Crucifixion of Our Lord and Saviour Jesus Christ, instead what we have to do is to try and accept PJ's death and to move on. We need first though to pay our dues to his life.

PJ was born in 1952 and baptised here in this church and he lived most of his life in this place. He was a gentle and kind man and it was his kindness and his softness and his gentleness that made the tragedies of his life so difficult to get over. And his life had its own upsets and difficulties and he did his best to keep going. He had (like everyone else) his own sorrows but he tried to make the best of things. He was religious too. God and the things of God were important to him. And that's why we can be confident that the God who gave him life will be good to him in his death, the God who knew the anguish of personal suffering in the person of his Son on Calvary will take PJ to himself by virtue of his Son's resurrection, the God who loved PJ in life will be able to put the jigsaw of his life together.

On an occasion like this when hearts are heavy with the pain of loss, there's the temptation to be overcome with grief and even despair, to become so bound up in the pain and suffering of this time so as to be blinded to the possibilities for goodness and for happiness and love that lie around us, to become so wrapped up in winter that we forget that spring is here, to become so immersed in crucifixion that we forget about the resurrection.

At times like this what we need, above all, is to ask God to deepen our faith in his goodness and mercy and love, to help us to understand that behind the unresolved mysteries of life, behind the contradictions and the strangeness of human living that there is a purpose, a reason, a meaning behind what appear to us in our restless way to be purposeless or indifferent. And this is where our faith comes in.

It comes in making the connection between the life PJ lived on this earth and the life with God we now believe he enjoys in heaven. It comes too in seeing that the work he did, the love he brought to his family, the goodness he could create for those around him, the fun too that despite his troubles he so often engendered, the neighbours he visited, the mark he made on his place and time - are all offered to God in his death.

And it comes too in reminding us that Jesus died for each one of us, that he has gone before us to prepare a place for each one of us so that we may share with him in his glorious resurrection.

We need to understand (vaguely though we often do) that behind the pain and the tears of this day there is a happiness that PJ believed God had prepared for all of us. But despite our faith and even with our faith death disrupts and diminishes our lives and we have to deal with that too. But Jesus has said 'Come to me all you who labour and are overburdened and I will give you rest. Shoulder my yoke and learn from me for I am gentle and humble of heart and you will find rest for your souls.'

On this sad occasion when the air is charged with a family's and a community's grief, let us place our trust and our hope in the arms of our loving Saviour. Jesus said 'Do not let your hearts be troubled, trust in God still and trust in me.'

So despite the pain of this day, despite the restlessness of spirit that we may feel, let us entrust PJ to the loving arms of the God in whose image he was made. Let us offer the joyful mysteries and the sorrowful mysteries of his life to the God who loved him in life and now cares for him in death. We pray that those who loved him dearly may be given the strength and the courage to cope with his death. And we pray especially that God may welcome him home to that great city the new and eternal Jerusalem.

FATHER'S DAY
Wearing your heart outside

I was reading the other day someone who was explaining the difference between knowledge and wisdom. A young man, he said, will drive a car at one hundred miles an hour because he knows he's not going to die, an older man will slow down because he knows he is. The point is that there are some things that we have to learn for ourselves. There are some things that only life can teach us.

Someone wrote somewhere that we can have the experience but we can miss the meaning. We can float through some of the most important and significant experiences of our lives and it's only in retrospect that we can milk the meaning from them.

I remember many, many years ago, when my father was ill, visiting him in hospital and I remember having to rush away because I was so busy, because I had so much to do. And I remember him saying to me on one occasion, 'Why don't you wait a while more.' And I did. I waited for a while but only for a while and then I dashed off to do whatever important things I had to do. He died a few days later and I often wondered afterwards whether on that particular day, whether there was something he might have wanted to say to me, whether we needed that space together to till for a final time that fertile piece of ground between father and son.

Now of course I'll never know. But what I do know now is how little I knew then, how immature and unthinking was my response, how deep the experience was and how much I missed the meaning.

We know it all, of course, when we're young. When we're young, death is something that happens in other families. When we're young fathers and mothers are immortal, they were always there and therefore we imagine that they will always be there. And sometimes we never really get around to saying the things that really matter and then we find ourselves around a hospital bed trying to get it all said, trying to put words on things we've never tried to put words on before. And we can't understand why we haven't the vocabulary to do it.

The relationship between a parent and child is full of meaning and is fraught with difficulty. Is there any experience in life that compares in significance with the parenting of a child? Is there anything people do that has such extraordinary long-term ramifications for the lives of those involved? Is there any human situation more complex than that space between parent and child?

I remember hearing Christy Kenneally say recently that having a child is like wearing your heart outside your body for the rest of your life. Wearing your heart outside your body for the rest of your life. It's like a life sentence in a way because for as long as you live everything in your life is placed in the context of your child.

I remember years and years ago being at a funeral of a young man who had died and it was a time when I knew so little about the experience that I felt I had to fill the silence with words. I found myself saying to the father of the young man. 'I know what you're going through.' And he looked at me very kindly but very clearly and he said. 'No, you don't, you have no idea what I'm going through.' And of course I hadn't. I thought knowledge was the same as wisdom.

It's a mistake that's often made. Believing we know, thinking we understand and then later on realising that we weren't even at the pictures. Isn't it a pity in a way that we have to experience so much to learn so little. But that's the way it is because, in this case, the cliche is actually true. Life is the great teacher and the things that really matter can only be learned with the heart.

And it takes a long time to come to that. And it takes a long time to understand that, as a matter of course, life for everyone is a great mixture of regret and failure. That's part of the human package, that's part of the way we function as human beings.

The difficulty is that the parameters of that bit of ground that a father and a child occupy together shift constantly as the relationship changes. When we're children everyone's Daddy is the best Daddy in the world. Then when we're teenagers, we discover that in fact my father - whatever about your father-hasn't really got a clue about anything. And then if we live long enough, and if we're lucky enough to have our fathers with us long enough to find out, we discover how rich and fertile that rood of ground is. We discover that what makes a father important and exceptional is the simple fact that as long as he has breath in his body he carries a flame of love in his heart. In Christy Kenneally's phrase, fathers, like mothers, wear their hearts outside their bodies every day they live.

On Father's Day, that's the key truth. After all God took the concept of a natural father, to help us to understand in some approximate way how much he loved us. So let us today praise our fathers living and dead. Let us thank God, our Father, for the gifts of life and love that they brought into our lives, for the work and the worry, the example and the warmth, for the bits and pieces that today surface warm and contented memories and loving feelings from our childhoods and not least for the faith and the hope and the love that they witnessed to often maybe in difficult and even depressing circumstances.

We know too that, as life is, every memory won't be warm, every feeling won't be good. We know too, that fatherhood has its sorrowful mysteries as well as its joyful mysteries. We know too that for some this Father's Day can have its regrets and pain and even anger.

But whatever it is for you, place it today on this altar and ask the God, who is everyone's loving father, to bring out of it whatever gratitude or healing or whatever it is that we, as sons and daughters, need on this day.

FIRST COMMUNION
A special day

TODAY is a special day for this faith-community, because today sixteen children will receive the Body of Christ for the first time. Our prayer today, as we gather as a community to celebrate this special day, our prayer today is that the faith, hope and love that makes this day possible for them, will take root in their hearts and souls and remain with them all the days of their lives.

There are many people in the world today who wouldn't understand or accept what's happening here. But for us, it's part of the natural order of things that children in our faith-community, who have reached a certain age of reason and understanding, would receive Communion for the first time. And it's part of the natural order of things because these children come from a community and, in the main, from families rooted in the faith, hope and love of Jesus Christ.

When these sixteen children were baptised, responsibility was taken for their growth in the faith by their parents and god-parents and indeed by the whole faith-community. Because it is the parents' and the godparents' and all our responsibility to help these and all our children towards a knowledge and a love of God.

Now I'd like to say a few words to the children: to Deirdre, Justin, Declan, Mary, etc.

When you were tiny babies, just a few days old, your Daddys and Mammys brought you to this church. The priest poured water on your forehead and he said, 'I baptise you in the name of the Father and of the Son and of the Holy Spirit.' And he took a candle and he lit it from the Easter Candle - a candle like this candle I have here in front of me - and he gave it to your Mammys and Daddys to hold for you because your hands were too small to hold it for yourself. And that candle stood for Jesus who loved you then and who loves you now. And your Daddy and Mammy were told to keep that candle for you so that when you got older you could hold that candle for yourself, to remind you of how much Jesus loves you. And that candle is here lighting on this altar today, reminding you again of how much Jesus loves you in giving himself to you in Communion today.

So today is a special day not just for you but for your Daddys and Mammys and for your brothers and sisters and Grannys and Grandas too. They are delighted with how much you have grown up since the day they brought you into this church as a baby for baptism. They are delighted with how you made your first Confession. And they will be delighted later on in this Mass when you receive your first Holy Communion.

So today is a very special day, not just because of the lovely dresses and suits you have and not just because later on you will receive presents. No, today is important because for the first time in your life you will receive the body of Jesus into your growing body as food and nourishment for your life. And, please God, you will continue all through your life to receive the body of Jesus as food and nourishment on your journey through life.

To your Daddys and Mammys I say, 'Well done for the love and care and support you have given your children. On their behalf and on behalf of our faith-community I say thanks to you for bringing your children up in the faith, for helping to give them a sense of God and the things of God and for encouraging them to see a God who loves them and cares as an enrichment of their lives now and in the future.'

Today our prayer is above all a prayer of thanks to God, focussed on this Eucharist, thanks for all he has done for your children and for your families: for health of mind and body; for care and for comfort; and for faith, hope and love.

May God bless these special children on this special day and may the light of faith, hope and love that burns brightly for them today burn brightly for them all the days of their lives.

GRADUATION MASS
Letting go

WHEN I was a child one of the most annoying experiences of my life was when visitors would come to the house and remark on how much we'd grown since they had seen us last – as if we were a line of pot-plants. Then they'd start a long conversation about whether we resembled my father's people or my mother's people. I had to stand there and endure this long discussion about whether my nose or my chin resembled that of my Uncle Jack or my Aunt Mary or both. It used to annoy me intensely because as far as I was concerned I wasn't like my Uncle Jack or my Aunt Mary.

But of course I was completely wrong. Because like everyone else I didn't just drop out of the sky. I was - physically and emotionally and in so many other ways - what my family and my circumstances had made me. I was part of the present but I was also part of the past. And the past as much as the present was conspiring to make me what I was.

In other words, whether we like it or not, we are shaped and defined by our past. Teachers see it in the first-year class on the first day of school. A face in the crowd rings a bell and a teacher wonders is that young girl someone's sister in fourth year or, if you're long enough in school, even someone's daughter from a few years back.

We all know the experience. You go back to your own place and the faces of people have a familiarity about them. They echo the faces of other people and other years.

I recently had the experience of hearing my nephew speak and it took me a long time to realise that what was familiar about his voice was that it had an uncanny resemblance to my father's, his grandfather's. We pick up the accents and inflections of our voices from the voices around us, even when we don't realise that we do. And of course we pick up more than accents.

We pick up values and attitudes, ideas and feelings, appreciations and prejudices, an understanding of life and of people, skills of communicating and learning, a variety of thoughts that reflect the lives we have lived, the people we have met, the circumstances through which we have been shaped. And out of that confusion of emotions and feelings, values and attitudes, people and places, we discover certain truths. We come to certain conclusions about life and about living, about what is important and what is not that important.

And in all of this there is a searching and a sifting. A searching for a sense of our own worth and dignity, a searching out of respect for ourselves and for others, a searching for an experience of being loved and of loving, a searching for real and true friendship, a search for God.

There is a sifting too – a sifting of priorities, a sifting of attitudes, a sifting of relationships, a sifting of values around which you will shape your life. There is, as Ecclesiastes reminds us, a time to be born, a time to die, and there is too, a time for searching and a time for sifting.

There is too a time for letting go, not letting go of the past as if it can be just thrown away, as if somehow we could leave it out with the refuse. Because we can't throw it away even if we wanted to. But a letting go nonetheless of many of the bits and pieces of childhood and adolescence, the many and varied props that were necessary for our growth and development but that we now need to shed.

Just as a little child lets a mother's hand go and ventures to make her first faltering steps, just as the growing child lets go of the security of a father's hand in order to swim, to cycle or to do the one-hundred and one things that growing up demands, so too this graduation marks a letting go, so that life will be formed and shaped for the future.

And this letting go is full both of pain and full of promise. There is the pain of parents letting go, that difficult pain that is necessary for trust and for independence. There is the pain of leaving behind the security and the stability of home. There is the pain of setting out into a new world with all the risk and the worry that entails.

But there is the promise too - the promise of life's voyage moving on to another stage, the promise of growth, the promise that, in hope and in prayer, the future holds. And hope above all is what is at the very heart of voyage and of journey. And hope above all is the note that we all need to strike today.

Hope isn't a kind of pious wish that everything, in the best fairy-tale tradition, that everything will turn out well and everyone will live happily ever after. No! Hope is a recognition that life is no fairytale, that things do go wrong, that the world we live in is not always for everyone the clean, healthy place that we would like it to be, that pain and suffering, in one form or other, are part of the hand that life deals to us.

But what hope says is that despite the darker side of life, despite the trials and the difficulties that life always throws up, hope says that despite it all, you move forward to another stage of life's journey, confident in your abilities and in the way those abilities have been shaped in this school, confident in the legacy of love and security that your homes have provided, confident in a God who, as Isaiah reminds us, has called each one of us by name and who holds each one of us in the hollow of his hand.

So this evening as we mark the graduation of the Leaving Certificate class of this year, we pray for that sense of hope to remain with you in the years ahead and we place the future of this class in the protective arms of God. My wish, the wish of your teachers, the wish of your parents is that you may live up to your abilities and to your ambitions, that you may live up to the love and concern your parents have for you and for your future, that you may live up to the ideals that have been set before you in this school. I wish you this evening everything you wish yourselves . . . life, health, happiness. When you look back on this day may you think fondly on home and on school and on all those who brought you this far. May God be with you wherever the great voyage of life takes you.

OPENING MASS OF SCHOOL YEAR
A new beginning

The beginning of a new school year brings to our minds a whole range of attitudes and emotions. For first years there's the excitement of a new phase of life - new classrooms, new teachers, different subjects, new friends. For the second years there's a new confidence born of the feeling that they are no longer (if you like) the babies of the school. The third years, of course, have the Junior Cert to attend to at the end of the year - so there is an extra focus to their year. For transition years the expression 'laid back' often seems the most appropriate and even the word 'doss' becomes a favourite expression. For the fifth years, there's the relief that the Leaving Cert is still some way away. And then there are the Leaving Certs who are sometimes defined as 'those students who regret the way they spent last year.'

For the Leaving Certs of course there is the pressure of the big exam at the end of the year, relief that the end of school is in sight, worries about decisions to be made and places in college or in employment to be secured, doubts about the future - a whole series of conflicting emotions and attitudes.

Now put all that group of young people into the same building for six hours a day for two-hundred days a year; remind yourself that all of those young people are going through what everyone agrees is the most difficult part of their lives - growing up, finding themselves, establishing their own identities or whatever; put them with a group of teachers who like everyone else will have their good days and bad days; and what you might expect is a recipe for disaster.

But the extraordinary thing of course is that in the whole

history of the human race no one has as yet devised a better system of coping with the education of young people. It's not a perfect system but it's the best we've got and like every other system that's less than perfect those who do best with it are those who put most into it. So you could say that today in this Mass we have as our theme - 'Back to the Future', a sense that we are all back after the long summer holidays and that what lies ahead during the coming year is the future for all of us. There is some of that future that we can control; there are decisions we can take and live out that will shape that future; but there is part of that future that we simply can't control - part of it that is literally in God's hands.

And that's why we're here this morning to place our lives and our future in God's hands - to ask God to give us the courage and the strength and the confidence to shape that future by living up to whatever responsibilities we have in this school for this year. And also to accept before God that much of our lives this coming year, much of the maturing and growing and developing that we hope will happen will depend on his sustaining love for all of us. And because the God we believe in, the God Jesus Christ taught us about, because that God is a God of love and mercy and goodness - because God is God - we can with hope and confidence look forward to what this year will bring.

Every dream doesn't come true – all of us are old enough to realise that – and sometimes dreams have a peculiar way of turning out to be quite different from what we expect.

So let me finish with a short story which is appropriate in the circumstances:

Once upon a time in a forest, three young trees were growing side by side. As they grew, they shared with one another their dreams of what they would become when they grew to be big trees.

The first tree said, "My dream is to become part of a luxurious home where many famous people come and go and admire the grain and texture and colour of my wood."

The second tree said. "My dream is to become the tall mast of an elegant sailing ship that journeys to the seven seas."

And the third said. "My dream is to become part of a great

41

tower, so high that it will inspire people who look at it. People will come from all over the world to see it.'

And so the young trees dreamed.

Eventually the trees grew to maturity and were cut down. The first didn't become a part of a luxurious home, as it had dreamed, but instead some of its wood was fashioned into a simple manger that one day cushioned a baby in swaddling clothes.

The second tree didn't become the tall mast of an elegant ship, as it had dreamed, but instead it became the sides of an ordinary fishing boat like many others on the Sea of Galilee.

The third tree didn't become part of a tall tower, as it had dreamed, but was fashioned into the beams of a cross and used for a crucifixion.

We don't know what this new year will bring. We can't predict the twists and turns of life. We know that there are some things we can make happen, some dreams we can make come true. But we know too that all the bits and pieces of the jig-saw of this year and of the lives we will all lead are ultimately in God's hands. May we have the health and the strength and the conviction to do what we can do during this year and may we have the faith to leave the rest in God's hands.

SCHOOL CENTENARY
Remembering with gratitude

N OSTALGIA, as the saying goes, isn't what it used to be. Of
course, nothing is, what it used to be. We live and we
change. We change and we live. And, hopefully, in the process, we
grow a bit too. To live, a saint said one time, is to change, and to
live well is to change often.

But for all that, we know we cannot shed the past. It's part of
what we are now and still part, too, of what we are becoming. We
are, in many ways, beneficiaries of our past, and we are,
unfortunately sometimes, the prisoners of it too.

But, like it or not, to a greater or lesser degree, we are what
our past has made us. We have been honed and shaped and
formed by a mixture of influences and experiences. Like the kiln
in a pottery, the grain and the texture of the clay that are part of
the very fibre of our being have been heat-baked into an
unchanging and unchangeable mass. The influences and
experiences of our early days are a kind of oven in which the
shape of what we are becomes permanent.

So the past is there within us. And so, from time to time, we
find that the memories come flowing back: a pair of horses
pulling a plough on a crisp spring day with a swarm of busy
seagulls hanging in the surrounding air; a woman returning
from a shopping trip to town, two bags hanging precariously on
the handles of a bicycle; a copy of the Western People spread out
on the kitchen table; digging the new potatoes; repairing a
puncture on a bicycle tyre at the side of a road; and the teacher
at the blackboard in the old national school.

More than forty years on, the memories seem as fresh as they
ever were. Especially about primary school, the only educational

43

institution so many in the past attended. So the memories are crystal clear, like a spring well on a bright summer's day.

So we remember the long journey to school even though it was less than a mile; the schoolbags on our backs; the occasional diversion for sweets to O'Grady's when the pennies were flush; hair dampening despite our sheltering from the rain; sticking big toes in the melting tar on the hottest of summer's days; the laughter, the fun and, sometimes too the tears, that went to make up a fondly-remembered childhood; and Mrs Bourke waiting patiently for the scholars to settle before the day's work began.

For many people, Carrowgun National School was the first break with the security of home, an adventure out into the big world but with always the knowledge that, all things being equal, it was a home away from home. The worries and the frets of childhood were ministered to as we were introduced to the wonders of the basics of our education.

Looking back it seems a completely different world now with that mixture of innocence and acceptance that seemed to run through all of Irish life. Television hadn't arrived; videos hadn't been invented; magazines meant *The Far East* and *Africa*; and excitement was measured out in small portions. Little happened but when it did we subjected it to forensic examination. Little changed and we expected little to change. The past was an inheritance we had to understand because it wouldn't differ from either the present or the future. Life was the way it was and nothing, apart from the seasons, would ever change.

But change did come to disturb the tranquillity of our childhoods. And gradually we moved on but the memories lingered. But somehow we are always faithful to the food of our youth. And I hope we will be. The world may be a different place, the problems more complicated but the simple truths learned in home and in school continue to shape our paths to this day. Everything changes but everything, in a deeper sense, remains the same. The old order changeth (and thank God too for some of the change) giving way to new. A newly renovated school, extra teachers, better facilities another generation of children with their own dreams and eventually too their own memories, memories to savour and, in truth too, memories to let slip into the distant shadows.

In years to come the past for them will be, as it is for us, a memory to savour and to share. They too like us will bring to their remembering, the tinted spectacles that time seems to give us all. And that's no harm too because the mind has a way of sparing us the sharp edges of our memories. But whatever sharpness there is or there was will soon disappear as soon as the reminiscing starts and in the respectful silence that follows butterflies of acceptance and gratitude will come to rest on our shoulders.

One hundred years on, we remember our first academy, Carrowgun N.S., and all who walked those special years with us, with great fondness and with much gratitude.

A SCHOOL REUNION
Memories are made of this

I remember it as vividly as if it was yesterday. And I know that as long as I live it will be forever burned into my consciousness. My father (God rest him) met the headmaster and my brother gave me the grand tour. I was shown the big dormitory, the refectory, the handball alleys, the playing fields and last but not least that peculiar edifice of less-than-fond memory, what we called 'the Jacks.'

We were shown to our class-rooms - 1A and 1B at the end of the new wing – and we were introduced to the intricacies of Latin and Greek, the mysteries of Algebra and Geometry and later that first day to a football match on the Bottom Pitch.

It was of course a long time ago. Greek has gone, Latin has disappeared, 1A and 1B classrooms are gone, the bottom pitch has gone and even the infamous Jacks has disappeared.

But it was a long time ago - and today we approach it in memory. The truth, someone said, is fabled by the daughters of memory. What we actually remember comes to us not just through the sieve of twenty-five or thirty years but through the experiences we went through *then* and the experiences we've had *since*. And not just the experiences but what we did with them, how we handled them, and what they mean to us.

Not everyone has come back for this reunion. Some didn't make it because they couldn't be here. Others didn't make it not because they couldn't but because they didn't want to. And we have to respect that.

Memories after all differ. Some are very conscious of the friendships formed, the fun we had, the football we played, the matches we went to and so on. Others maybe have different thoughts. Some hurts heal more easily than others.

Satisfactions don't always register equally on the same human graph. It was a long time ago and for some it's painful to remember the past. What they feel and what we feel may be quite different but either set of feelings is as real and as authentic as the other. I can only talk about my own feelings.

And the first feeling I have today is one of gratitude. It cost the great sum of £70 a year to be a boarder here and if that education wasn't available at that price I would never have been able to get to secondary school. So I at least owe my old *alma mater* that.

A second feeling I have has to do with gratitude too - a gratitude for the sense of independence it gave me, a sense that if you can take care of yourself in boarding school you can take care of yourself anywhere. I feel too a sense of gratitude for the fun and the excitement that filled my adolescent school days, the friendships that deflected us (boarders) from the deprivations of home and the limitations of the refectory menu.

I remember the irregular outings to the pictures in the Savoy and the big question always was, 'is it in technicolour or black and white?' I remember the football pilgrimages to Sligo and Ballaghaderreen (where we competed with other concentration camps called St Nathys and Summerhill) and the big question (for us boarders at least) was not 'Will we win the match'? but 'Will we get the dinner?'

I remember the plays - the drama on and off the stage, the highly improbable leading ladies and the trips up and down to the Town Hall. I remember the day-boys bringing in packets of Goldgrain for one shilling and three pence and, if you had a few pence extra, a packet of Jacobs Milk Choc.

There are other memories too that I don't particularly want to call to mind: the times maybe when we weren't treated as well as we might have been, the incidents that maybe have left a sour taste in many a mouth and last but by no means least the limited menu that graced the refectory table.

Maybe it's a bit unfair to be critical - it is after all easy to be critical in retrospect.

But even though we sometimes falsely imagine that we're still in our prime after all these years, 1961-1966 was a long, long time ago. Television hadn't arrived, videos hadn't even been invented, cars meant the Ford Prefect and the Consul, everyone (or practically everyone) was a Pioneer, no one doubted the existence of God.

It was, as someone said about a different time, it was the best of times and it was the worst of times but, for better or for worse, it has shaped and formed us into what we are today.

So let's us give thanks for this school and for the years we spent here and let us ask forgiveness too for the hurts or the failings of that time. The old order has changed. It has given way to new and the more it drifts into the past maybe the more tinted the spectacles we bring to it, the less important the deprivations seem to be.

That's probably the way life is anyway. Whatever hurts or deprivations we bring with us from school or childhood, life somehow consumes them and in the years that follow acceptance and gratitude tend to come. I hope we feel something approaching acceptance and gratitude today and I hope too that those who don't will find it some day.

JUBILEE OF CHURCH
Our sacred space

W E have come together today to celebrate the silver jubilee
of the building of this church. On the threshold of a new
century and a new millennium it might seem that twenty-five
years is too short a time for remembering, it might seem that a
span of twenty-five years doesn't demand or deserve a
commemoration.

But of course what we're commemorating is not just a
building that was put up twenty-five years ago, what we're
commemorating is the faith that built this church, the faith that
sustains this church. We're commemorating a sacred place at the
heart of this community. We're commemorating a still centre in
our community devoted to worshipping our God.

Before the building of this church there was the old church
built on this site. It was built in 1825 and it was the still centre
of the faith of this community for almost one-hundred and fifty
years. Before that there were Mass centres in different places.
There was the Penal Day Church in Leaffoney which was in use
in the early 19th century; there was the Chapel Field in Glann
where Bishop Bellew confirmed a large number of people -this
was sometime between the end of the eighteenth century and the
beginning of the nineteenth century, sometime between the years
1780 and 1812; there was a Mass House in Quigabar and there
was the church in the old Kilglass Cemetery where people
gathered to worship during the Middle Ages.

So what we're celebrating is a faith that extends back into the
mists of past centuries, a faith that is, thank God, still vibrant in
this community as we enter another millennium.

This church is our sacred place now. This is the place where we worship as a faith community; where new members of God's family are welcomed in baptism; where our children growing in faith go to Confession and Communion for the first time; where our young people are confirmed in their faith in the sacrament of Confirmation; where couples exchange their vows in the Sacrament of Marriage; where we bring our dead as we pay our last respects in the rituals of Christian death and burial; where God calls us to be. This is the (still) centre of our faith, where the sanctuary light continues to burn, as a sign of God's presence among us.

So it's right that we should remember with joy and with pride the faith that has fuelled the life of this community going back the long and difficult centuries of our history. We should remember those who kept the flame of faith alive; those who gathered in windswept and rainswept valleys to attend Mass during the Penal Days; those who provided out of their minimal resources a house for God's people to worship in; those who came to Mass, who said their prayers, those too who have long since died, the people who knelt in these seats and in the seats of the old Kilglass Church, those who said their prayers and gave their families a sense of God and the things of God; and not least those who 30 years ago set about building a new church in this special place.

So we remember today the faith, hope and love that made this church possible. We remember those who were on the church committee; those who organised the different collections; those who contributed to the various fund-raising events, the plays and the concerts and the dances; those who contributed from overseas; and all who, in any way, made any contribution to the building of this church. So it's right that we should remember Canon Paddy Maloney and all those who have left us this fine church.

But our remembering isn't just a mere remembering. It's not a nostalgic revisiting of times past. Our remembering is also about preparing, preparing for another generation to carry the flame of faith into a new century and into a new millennium.

So we don't just look back in gratitude and in pride at the faith that has sustained our community over the centuries, we look forward in faith and in hope into the future. And that's why part of our remembering has been to look at our church and to see how we might prepare this building for worship in the next century.

In the commemorative booklet which we have prepared for this evening there's a photograph of Canon Michael Munnelly saying Mass in the old church and John Carden, the sacristan, serving the Mass. It was the old Mass, as so many of us remember it. It was in Latin. Canon Munnelly had his back to the people. It was a Mass that people attended rather than participated in.

It was a Mass that many people look back on very fondly, and it was a Mass that for generations sustained the faith of our people. But I'm convinced that awesome and sacred and full of mystery as that Mass was, it would not now sustain the faith of our people.

For our faith to be sustained, for that flame of faith to be carried into a new century we need a liturgy that engages the whole person. We need a worship that engages not just the mind and the intellect but the senses and the feelings. And that's why in preparation for the new century that's why we have decorated our church and reformed the sanctuary.

So as part of our remembering as a faith community we have created this place where we can bring to bear all the gifts of our community into our worship and into our liturgy in the hope and in the promise that we will both deepen and sustain our own faith and help a new generation to find their faith in their way, in their own time and in this, their own place.

So we are grateful this day for all those who have walked the pilgrim path before us, for all the priests and the religious who have served this faith-community, for all those who have come to this church and to the churches and mass-centres before it over the years and have kept the flame of faith burning brightly.

That flame carries with it both a privilege and a responsibility. It is a great privilege to be part of a vibrant faith-community but we have a responsibility too to bring that faith - intact, active and real - into the next century. That's why we celebrate this jubilee this day. It is our celebration of our faith as we face another century. May God be with us on another stage of life's journey.

51

ORDINATION DAY
A vision of eternity

IN a few moments John will be ordained a priest of God,
symbolised by the laying on of hands. In a few moments he
will resolve to live, to work and to pray as a priest of Jesus
Christ for the rest of his earthly life, promising obedience to his
bishop and his successors, accepting the vow of celibacy he has
already taken and praying that through God's goodness, the
encouragement of his family and friends and the support of his
brother priests that what will be begun here today, may be
completed in God's own time.

But to understand what is happening here today, we have to
look into the future and into the past: forward, to the life John
will lead and the work he will do, and back into the past too, to
understand what it all means.

Back not just to the great sacramental moments of his life: his
baptism when he first became part of the priesthood of Jesus
Christ; or his first Communion when he received the Body of
Christ for the first time; or his Confirmation when he accepted
the promises made for him by his parents and sponsors in
baptism; or the more recent past when he received the
preparatory orders of priesthood.

No - important and all as these occasions are, we have to go
much further back than that. Back to the time when a man
walked this earth, a man whom we believe to be God the Son,
the Second Person of the Trinity, the one who came to reveal God
to us, to show us what God was like, to help us understand why
we are alive, how we should live and how your life and mine fit
into the vast tapestry of God's design for our world.

And he called the apostles to continue his work on earth of

preaching his gospel of faith, hope and love. And his followers bound themselves together in a community of love, which came to be known as the Church, as the community of God's family. And the apostles ordained priests to help them with God's work.

And as a continuing part of that great human and spiritual process, that great pilgrimage of God's people, the bishop as a successor to the apostles will in a few moments ordain John to priesthood.

It is a service for which he has been called as Jeremiah was called in the first reading - 'Before I formed you in the womb I knew you . . . before you were born I consecrated you . . .' 'You did not choose me' St. John tells us in the gospel 'but I chose you.' And St. Paul reminds us that God makes his own choice for his own good reasons.

And just as God promised a reluctant Jeremiah that he would be at his side so we can be confident that in the years ahead of John's priestly service the God who in the gospel said, 'No longer do I call you servants, I call you friends', the God of Jesus Christ will be with him to empower him and to sustain him.

And as in the life of every other priest that empowering and that sustaining will be needed.

John's ordination today and his commitment to priesthood and the gospel values that underpin it, are what Vatican Two said religious life should be, a sign to the world, a sign which reminds each and every one of us that we have not here a lasting city, but that we all journey towards one. And we need that sign.

We need that witness. We need the witness of the priesthood and the religious life to make us question the easy choices we so often make, to make us unhappy with the easy compromises of our lives, to jolt us out of the cult of mediocrity that can imprison us so easily.

In a world that seeks pleasure almost at any cost, we need the witness value of a generous and joyful living of a life of chastity. In a world of creeping materialism, a world which practically canonises affluence and excess, we need the witness of people who seek freedom from the pull of material possessions.

In a world where authority is breaking down, where people insistently want to have their own way, we need the witness of people who are prepared to accept direction and guidance not because it's always right but for the good of the Church and for

the service of God's people. It isn't easy to face into a doubtful future. It isn't easy to cope with a changing and an increasingly secular world. It isn't easy to be a very polite Christian for the rest of your life.

And yet that again is the life and task of the priest - that and much more. We will pour water over babies in the sometimes uncertain hope that they will grow up to be Christian. We will listen in a dark confessional to the sins of the faithful. We will struggle to ease painful exists from this world with some semblance of meaning and dignity. We will be privileged to bend over a wafer of bread and a cup of wine and to transform them by a simple expression of words into the body and blood of our Lord and Saviour. We will be expected, despite our doubts and limitations, to make God a bit more tangible for our people, to bring a vision of eternity to the ordinary lives of the people entrusted to our care.

On this occasion of grace, our prayer is that the strong faith that nourished John in his own home, the love of his family, the support of his friends, the respect of his teachers and above all his own commitment and enthusiasm will help him to serve faithfully and well whatever community of God's people will be entrusted to his care.

To whatever part of God's vineyard John will be assigned, in whatever form is the ministry to which he is called in God's Church, wherever his own pilgrimage of faith will lead, may he allow his future to be shaped according to God's redeeming plan. And may God bless him with life, health and happiness and above all with the commitment and energy to do his work in the vineyard of the Lord.

JUBILEE OF ORDINATION
Songs and promises

There's a song that Tommy Makem used to sing called *The Parting Glass*. It's about a man who at the end of his days 'weeps for all the songs he didn't sing and the promises he didn't keep.' It's a song about that difficult mixture of regret and longing and while it doesn't reflect my experience of the last twenty-five years of priesthood, there's something of that in it too. In a way, every life is about *songs* and *promises*, the songs we sing and those we don't sing, the promises we keep and those we don't keep. And out of the songs and the promises of our lives we quarry our own individual and unique existence in this world.

So in marking twenty-five years of priesthood I'm thanking God for the songs and the promises of the last twenty-five years and I'm looking forward with hope and confidence to the songs and promises of the years to come. And part of that marking is looking back to my ordination day in my native parish, back to the people who gathered to celebrate that day with me, to those still to the good as we say, and to those who have died.

But I look back too not just to an ordination day twenty-five years ago, back not just to the faith community that my native parish was for me, back not just to the faith community that home and family were for me. I look back too to my Baptism and my first Confession and my first Communion and my Confirmation. And important and all as these events were for me personally, I need to look back much further than that, to understand what ordination or priesthood mean.

I look back to the time when a man walked on this earth to show us what God was like and to help us understand qualities

like truth and mercy and freedom and forgiveness and love, to help us understand what these meant and what they could mean for us and for our world.

That man I believe was God, and he brought together a very disparate group of people who continued his work on this earth. And his followers bonded themselves into a community, the community of God's family, what we now call the Church. And out of that community individuals were called and are called to minister as priests to God's family.

That, if you like, is where the songs and the promises of my life come in. There was a call, and I remember it graphically. There was an answer and there is a priesthood. And for the last twenty-five years, that priesthood has brought me to five different parishes and it was in those places that the songs and the promises of priesthood found whatever expression they found.

Someone said once that priesthood, like religious life, is a sign of a melody beyond the ordinary song that we sing and it's a sign of a promise beyond the ordinary commitment that we give. I'm not too sure about that because there's always the temptation to turn religion into piety, to turn priesthood into something so extraordinary and so holy that we forget that it's ultimately an ordinary person living an ordinary life.

And those who struggle to live it are no better or no worse than others. Those who are priests are priests not because they just *want* to be but because in some peculiar sense they feel they *have* to be. Because that call of priesthood, that call of inconvenience and unreason is just *there* for some people and not answering that call is almost not living life at all.

Priesthood is about a lot of things that shape us and that we shape but, at the end of the day, priesthood is about witness. Words are important, of course, and priests use a lot of them but words, as we say, can be cheap and people may choose to believe them or not but no human word reaches the depths to which real witness goes.

And this is one of the frightening things about priesthood, about actually being a priest. People look to me and to every other priest as if qualities and values like truth and right living and holiness come automatically, as if the frailties of the human condition are not applicable to those who happen to be priests. As if somehow priests have some magic formula, some special grace that inoculates us against the limitations and the failures of the rest of the human race.

Believe me, when I was ordained twenty-five years ago, when the bishop anointed me with oil or laid hands on me, it didn't change me in any way. I was the same three and tuppence as I was the day before. But what was different was that I was given a responsibility and an authority to attend in witness and in service to those given to my care. What was different was that I was given and accepted a ministry of God's presence in the world. And what that means in simple language is that it's my work as a priest to help open up the presence of God to people. And this isn't something that's neat and packaged. This isn't about having ready answers or neat solutions to the messiness of life. This is about mystery. This is ultimately about standing humbly before our God in wonder and in awe, trying to grasp something of the whiff of God through our own experience and our own living, through what God has said to us in the scriptures, through what God is saying to us in our own lives. This is about trying to plot a track for the kind of life that God calls each one of us to live.

It's not about knowing all the answers; it's not about knowing better than anyone else; it's about opening up, one hopes delicately and respectfully, a window into God's world. That's what priesthood is and I thank God for the last twenty-five years of priesthood - for the songs that have been sung and for the promises that have been kept. And, like the singer of *The Parting Glass*, I too weep for all the songs I didn't sing and the promises I didn't keep.

I think that's part of it too, part of the story of my life and of every life, the regrets that if we're honest are always just below the surface of the rest of our lives, the words I should have said and didn't say, maybe too the words I shouldn't have said and did say, the times when selfishness or failure or fear or sin limited or dulled the presence of God rather than opening up the presence of God. This may not be the worst of times for Church and for priesthood but it's certainly not the best of times either. When I was ordained twenty-five years ago the bright promise of the Second Vatican Council was lifting hearts and minds and morale among priests was very high. We had the wind on our backs. The

Church and everything it stood for was granted at least a hearing on every platform of substance.

Now things are different, morale is low, fewer are going on for priesthood, that great pedestal that priests were on when I was ordained twenty-five years ago is now in bits around our feet. And I'm happy that it is because a pedestal is absolutely the last place a priest should be. And even though I obviously regret the great scandals that have rocked the Church in recent years, even though I obviously regret the terrible pain that has been visited on so many, particularly young children and even though it's painful to acknowledge the diminishment of priesthood that all that awfulness has brought with it, I sense too a new reality dawning for the church and for priesthood. I sense a new freshness, a new humility, a new respect based not on position or privilege or elitism of any kind but based on an acceptance of our vulnerable humanity in the face of life's difficulties.

In years to come there will be other songs that we will need to sing and other promises we'll need to keep. But maybe now we'll do it with a bit more humanity and a bit more humility.

So I look forward to working as a priest in the years ahead. I look forward to respectfully ministering to the presence of God in this place; to the privilege of accepting children into God's family at baptism; to the privilege of administering in the confessional God's pardon and God's peace; to the privilege of doing what I can to ease painful exits from this world with a dignity and a graciousness that as a people you have a right to expect; to the privilege of standing at this altar and bending over a wafer of bread and a cup of wine to change them into the body and blood of our Lord and Saviour as food for God's people; to continuing, despite my failures and my limitations, to try to make God a bit more tangible and to help bring a vision of eternity to the lives of the people entrusted to my care.

So I thank God for the songs and promises of the last twenty years and I pray for the songs that have still to be sung and the promises that I still need to keep. I thank God too for all those who have walked the last twenty-five years with me - for my family, my friends, and for the parishioners of the five faith communities I have served over the past twenty-five years.

For all that has gone I give thanks and I ask pardon; for whatever is to come, I place, on this day, in God's hands.

JUBILEE OF RELIGIOUS PROFESSION
Pilgrimage, poetry and presence

GATHERING is at the heart of Christian worship. We gather as a faith-people to worship, to break the Word of God, to break the bread of life, to enter into Communion around a common table. We can describe all of these activities in different ways but the word 'celebrate' is probably the best word to use.

Now sometimes, of course, that word 'celebrate' can seem forced and awkward but today, the word 'celebrate' couldn't be more apt to describe what we're doing here. Because what we're doing is celebrating the life of Sr Mary Jo, celebrating the faith that she found in her home in Carrowgun, celebrating the call of God to religious life and to mission, celebrating the work she has done over the last fifty years, and last, but by no means least, celebrating the person, the woman, whom we all know as Mary Jo.

The Celtic monks saw life as pilgrimage, as poetry and as presence. Pilgrimage for them wasn't a journey to a particular place but an attitude that embraces all of life. In faith terms, pilgrimage takes the bits and pieces of our lives and places them within the context of a belief in a God who knows us and cares for us beyond all our imagining. And out of that conviction things happen to us and we make things happen, that constitute a lived life.

For Mary Jo, pilgrimage started in her home in Carrowgun. Her baptism, first Confession, first Communion, entry into religious life, first profession and final profession were markers on her life's pilgrimage. And now after more than forty years working on the mission-field there is a certain symmetry about returning to her own place and a certain aptness too about the ending of a particular phase of her life's pilgrimage.

The poetry of Mary Jo's life has to do with the kind of person she is, particularly the invariably benign and gentle disposition that she enjoys. In 1948 when she entered religious life for her formation, it seems, certainly in retrospect, and from what we hear, a very difficult, demanding even forbidding experience.

The poet, Sean Dunne, once said that religious life in the past was often a mixture of childishness and authoritarianism and while it's always dangerous to judge the past by the standards of the present, there is at least some evidence of how limited and inadequate religious formation tended to be. And I have no doubt too that in the long years of missionary service Mary Jo had some difficult times. And there was too, I'm sure, the deprivation of missing her brothers and sisters, missing the younger ones growing up especially during the first eleven years she spent in India without getting home for a visit. And yet, all her life, she has retained that gentleness and that benign spirit.

But even more than that I think she retains too a great sense of the joy of living life. There is a kind of glad engagement with the world, a fusion of the everyday and the holy that some people like Mary Jo are blessed with and it enables them to enjoy the good things of life as great blessings from God. And I hope no one will feel affronted if I say that it's not a noted characteristic among religious. The truth is that religious life has come out of a dense fog of legalisms and thou-shalt-nots that tended to divest people of their humanity and the essential joy that is at the very heart of life.

I think it's true to say that the Church in Ireland has become a much more human place in recent years, for a lot of different reasons, and one I think is that so many survived the problematic formation most of us received and came out the other end with their warmth and their humour and their sense of joy intact. They survived their religious formation the way our parents survived much of the nonsense that priests preached at them in the past. And they survived because of an innate belief in goodness, in personal happiness and particularly in the quality of life we describe as *joy*. That, I think, is the poetry the Celtic monks talked about.

Finally, the Celtic monks saw life as a presence. If you ask some people what a daffodil is, you'll get a lecture on botany and biochemistry, but no lecture, no series of chemical equations will ever describe the experience of seeing in the springtime that shape of yellow, burgeoning joy that we have experienced a daffodil to be.

And it isn't just the actual physical existence of a daffodil in spring. It has more to do with all the associations and all the experiences connected to it. It's about looking at a daffodil, not as a physical specimen but looking at it at an angle, seeing above and beyond it to the things that give it substance. And religious life is a bit like that. It's about living life at an angle to the world, it's about placing a question-mark against the world we live in, not in any contemptuous way, but accepting and embracing and loving the world God has given to us, and not being afraid to place question-marks against the prevailing wisdom of our time.

The writer, Flannery O'Connor, once said that the Church is the custodian of the sense of life as a mystery and the logic of that is that we must love our questions because it's the questions ultimately that birth the mystery. And ultimately too what makes religious life important is that it makes no sense. It makes no sense in economic or material terms; it makes no sense in interpersonal terms; it doesn't fit into any particular column of any balance-sheet. But it's there, a presence, looking at life from a particular angle, seeing things sometimes from a discomforting and awkward perspective, asking the difficult question, loving the awkward questions.

Religious life is about presence, a refining and joyful presence that seeks not to bludgeon people with the truth but rather to allow people to find that truth for themselves. The poet Seán Dunne said once that to experience the aroma of Christianity we must copy the rose. A rose doesn't preach at anyone. It simply spreads its fragrance and the rose irresistibly draws people to itself and the scent remains with them.

So today we thank God for the pilgrimage, the poetry and the presence that is the life that Mary Jo has lived, we thank God for the work she has done and continues to do, and above all we thank God for the person that she is and for that glad sense of engagement with the world which, please God, will remain with her all the days of her life.

LEAVING A PARISH
Final words

IT would, I feel, be inappropriate if I didn't say a few words on my last official weekend on duty here. The danger of course on an occasion like this is to become a bit dramatic or worse still sentimental. If I was going on the missions to the other end of the world and no-one would be likely to see me again, there would be some excuse for that but the fact that I'm just moving up the road a few miles should temper that particular approach.

I'm reminded too of a story of a priest who was leaving a parish and he told his congregation that they weren't to be too upset because the bishop had promised to send a good replacement. As he was leaving the Church he saw an old woman in tears and he said to her 'There's no need to cry, didn't the bishop say he would send a good replacement.' 'That's what I'm crying about' she said 'the bishop said the same thing before you came.'

So it's important to keep things in perspective.

What I want to say this morning is simply a word of thanks.

And I start of course by thanking God for the health of mind and body that he gave me while I was here. The next person in line with God is of course the parish priest so I have Fr X to thank as well. I regard his friendship as one of the great graces of my years here and I will treasure that friendship always.

There are many other people I would like to thank but I don't intend to get involved in listing names, for obvious reasons.

First of all I would like to thank the people (the sick and the elderly) whom I visited with Holy Communion on the First Fridays. I start with them because I am convinced that the greatest gift any people can give their priest is to support him in his faith and in his priesthood. And in the years I have spent here I have experienced in a special way that support from the sick and the housebound.

I would like as well to thank this congregation for the same reason, for being here weekend after weekend to celebrate your faith and my faith in our Lord and Saviour Jesus Christ. I would also like to thank the weekday congregation for their loyalty and faithfulness to their morning Mass. Their faith and your faith helped to support me in my faith and my priesthood and I appreciate that very much.

There are three groups that I particularly want to thank:

The first is the Parish Council, the members of which have worked over the years to facilitate the development and growth of the parish and to administer its varied aspects.

The second is the Parish Liturgy Group - for their perseverance and their patience and their efforts in trying to help this community in worshipping God in as complete and as rich a way as possible. For the meetings they attended, the risks they took, the sense of liturgy that they helped to generate in this community, for all of that and for them I am particularly grateful.

The third group is the choir or choirs and those who organise them and direct them. They are here in season and out of season and I want to thank them especially for being here at funeral Masses - to which they are so faithful.

I also want to thank all who helped out with the liturgy and parish activities - Mass servers, readers, lay ministers, the youth liturgy group, cleaners, ushers, those who take the bidding prayers, collectors, those who prepared the weekly bulletins, those who do the offertory procession, those who look after the decoration of the altar and the organisation of candles and so forth and not least those who opened and closed the Church.

I hope I have left no one out or that no one will feel left out of my thanks this morning. In case I have I want to take refuge in a general thank you.

In the years I have been here, I have shared much of life's uneven burdens with many families - the quiet satisfaction of the baptism of so many children; happy events like First Communion and Confirmation; the joy of wedding days; the sorrows of the deaths of so many old and indeed too (in my time here) so many young.

For whatever good I have done, for whatever service I have rendered, for what truth I may have witnessed to, I give thanks to God and to you this morning.

I hope too that I am sensible enough to realise that not everyone may be happy with what I've done or how I've done it, what I've said or how I said it. There's a story told of a priest who was moving from a parish and he ended up his final few words with the following, 'Jesus brought me to this parish and Jesus is moving me now to another parish.' And the choir, with whom he hadn't a particularly productive relationship, followed his final sentence with the hymn, 'What a friend we have in Jesus.'

One of the advantages of priests being moved fairly regularly is that for some people at least it is a blessing in disguise. There can be clashes of temperament, failures too on the part of the priest.

For any failure on my part, I ask understanding if not forgiveness. For any time when people's expectations of me as a priest have not been realised, I ask forgiveness for that too. I am very aware on this occasion of hopes not always having been fulfiled, of dreams not always coming true.

I have (after nearly five years here) my regrets as well as my consolations and both will become no doubt part and parcel of my life.

I hope at least I have covered the ground I need to cover in these words.

Finally, I thank you having me for the last five years. I am happy that so many have wished me well in my new work and wherever God's spirit will lead me.

I have no doubt but that as I look back on these years I will think fondly of you and it would be dishonest of me not to say that I hope too that you will think fondly of me. I hope I will be in your prayers as you will be in mine.

May God bless you all.

THE OLYMPIC SPIRIT
Accepting difference

THERE are different views of the Olympic story - the good, the bad, the ugly and the dangerous. But somewhere in the great Olympic mix is the lesson that sport has an extraordinary ability to bring people together, to bond athletes into one great sporting family, and to give us a sense of the extraordinary diversity and unity of the human family.

Almost every country in the world is represented - all shades of colours, politics and creeds. The five circles which make up the Olympic symbol represent the five continents and for once the logo tells the true story. There is, of course, a bleak side to it too: the drugs, the triumphal nationalism, the silly hype, the rampant commercialism.

Yet when the dust settles and the athletes perform, the questions and the cynicism soon disappear because the Olympic Games say something about the equality of all people from every corner of God's earth and the importance of accepting the great diversity that there is in the great human family. The message of the Olympics is that diversity is to be unambiguously cherished.

When the Olympic Games were held in Atlanta, there was a certain irony about the fact that Frank Barrett, a Traveller from Galway represented our country, represented, you could say, our acceptance of some of the diversity within our own country. I mention the word *irony* because behind the hype of Atlanta was the bitter truth that Frank Barrett's family lived in a halting site in Galway beside the municipal dump. What message do you give to a family if the only place their housing is acceptable is beside the town dump?

What do you say to a family whose son represents Ireland in

the greatest sporting occasion in the world but the country he represents didn't think his family is important enough to be given electricity? We were happy to have Frank Barrett representing us in Atlanta but when he was at home we didn't consider him worthy of the electric light. And isn't that the reality for us?

Not the hype of Sydney or Atlanta when we get into a tizzy about the extraordinary diversity of the human family and the recognition that everyone is made in God's image and that every human being deserves to be treated with respect and with dignity. But rather the reality on the ground is that, whatever about our grand thoughts about diversity, we insist often, not on cherishing diversity but, on making distinctions between people.

We thought the achievement of Atlanta would be Michelle Smith's gold medals but the real achievement of Atlanta may well be the fact that as a result of the Olympics and the hype that attended it, Frank Barrett's family now have the electric light in the halting site in Galway.

The real achievement of any Olympics, and particularly of the para-Olympics may be the reminder for all of us that every human being is made in the image of God. And a reminder too that that statement is a basic part of our faith as Christian people. We are all made in the image of God, regardless of the colour of our skin, or the social standing we enjoy or don't enjoy, regardless of whether we measure up or don't measure up to what society expects. And regardless of whether we're Sonia O'Sullivan winning a silver medal in Sydney or a disabled athlete coming last in a special race in a parish sports, each one of us is loved and cherished equally by God.

But we find it difficult to accept that. So difficult indeed that it's second nature to us to make distinctions, to draw a line in the sand that marks people off into acceptable or unacceptable categories. This human family of ours drew a line in the sand when six million Jews lost their lives in places like Dachau and Auswitz simply because they were Jews, because they weren't on the right side of some line.

This Church of ours drew a line in the sand when thousands of people were killed during the Inquisition because they didn't fit the pattern of what was acceptable at that time. The unborn child, the useless old person, the handicapped adult are in different ways on the wrong side of some line because on some social or economic scale they don't register a high enough count.

And every year the Dept of Education, on our behalf, draws a line to make distinctions between those who do or don't make the points grade in the Leaving Cert this year. And so often we do the same ourselves. We make distinctions, this area or that area, this family or that family, this kind of house or that kind of house, this kind of person or that kind of person.

And we all have our own scale on which we register the important counts: race, religion, colour, sex, politics, money or whatever. And we run the rule along another member of God's family, another human being made in God's image, to see if they come up to a certain social standard, to see if they can have the honour of living beside me or marrying into my family or are they even worth me bidding them the time of the day.

That sounds shocking and yet so many of us do that much of the time. And the reason is that we have accepted hook, line and sinker the parameters of respectability that the world has offered us: wealth, power, hygiene, politics, religion and so forth. And we dismiss the trouble-makers, the undesirables, those who don't fit.

So if you have money or if you're immaculately clean, or if you're a Catholic, or if you can speak the Irish language or dance an Irish jig at a crossroads or if you're the right political colour or if you're not in an irregular relationship, or if you haven't a child outside marriage, or whatever, then you fit, then you're respectable.

So how should we react to the tendency to draw the line? As Christians, as followers of Jesus Christ, we look at what Jesus did. And what he did was accept everyone regardless of their social or economic or other standing. He didn't reject the prostitute Mary Magdalene even though she was despised by the Pharisees. He didn't fire Peter, the designated leader of his Church, even though he was undependable in a crisis. He didn't even weed out Judas whom he knew was going to betray him.

The message is that making distinctions, creating divisions, justifying intolerance are all running counter to the Christian way. Accepting diversity, cherishing difference, respecting everyone, that's the way of Jesus Christ. Not drawing the line, not weeding out, not making a distinction.

ALL-IRELAND DAY
Living life to the full

IN the run up to the All Ireland final in 1989, Archbishop
Joseph Cassidy commented that when he saw the excitement
and the expectation generated by the possibility of a Mayo
victory, when he sensed the feeling of self-assurance and self
confidence and pride in the people around him, for the first time
in his life he felt he fully understood what the phrase from
Scripture meant, "And they shall renew the face of the earth."

Anyone driving through any part of Mayo this last week will
know exactly what he meant. The county is awash in a sea of red
and green. And there's only one subject anyone wants to talk
about. And what's extraordinary about it all is the lift it has
given to everyone. People seem to have a lightness in their step;
there's a confidence in the air; there's a great buzz around the
county.

Suddenly we've got a greater sense of who we are and where
we come from. There's a feeling of belonging, of being part of a
wider family. There's an extraordinary sense of a county identity
and solidarity that continues to surprise us.

And I think the first thing we have to do is to give thanks:
not just for all those whose dedication and ability make it all
possible but for the hope and the joy that have percolated
through the county in the last week. And for the joy and the
satisfaction that so many people have taken and are taking out
of the whole enterprise.

You can see it on the faces of young children. You can see it on
the faces of older people who are rediscovering the child in
themselves and the sense of adventure and joy that so many of
us thought we had left behind us. And suddenly Mayo is in the

All Ireland Final and we find ourselves waving red and green flags. And the experience isn't just about an All Ireland final or about Gaelic football. It goes much deeper than that. It's to do with the search for our own identity. It's about our own sense of place, and, above all, I think it's about the need in all of us to have a sense of joy and celebration in our lives.

Because it's only when you can really appreciate the gift that something is, it's only then that you can really, fully, enjoy it. And the truth of the matter is that for so many of us there is so little joy in our lives. That's a terrible thing for those trying to live a human life but it's even worse for those of us who are trying to live a Christian life.

Because if I'm trying to be a Christian person then the first thing I have to be is to be grateful for the gifts of God. And if I am truly grateful then I'll experience joy. And the awful and the terrible and indeed the shocking thing is that sometimes the last person you expect to be joyful is a religious person. In fact, some of the most depressing and joyless people you'll find are pious people. For them life is all agony in the garden and there isn't a hint of resurrection.

Now that's a complete and utter contradiction of what religion is. God has given us everything we have, the air we breathe, the health we enjoy, the people we love, the food we eat, the television we'll watch today's game on, the car we'll travel to Dublin in, and the hundreds of things we can enjoy in the modern world. And on top of that he came among us and he died for our sins. Every sin you have committed and I have committed, every sin you will ever commit and every sin I will ever commit, all wiped away, completely and forever and on top of all of that he's promised us the happiness of Heaven.

And instead of our hearts bursting with joy, so many holy and religious and pious people are depressed and disillusioned and, the sort of people – if you have any sense – you'd want to keep as far away from as possible. The sort of people who wouldn't know what joy is if it shook hands with them in the street.

Religious people by definition should be full of joy, full of beans, full of life. 'I came', Jesus said, 'so that you may have life and live it to the full.' And instead of that what do we often get? Lamentations, lamentations and more lamentations. Complaints about the state of the world, as if every ageing generation in the whole history of the world didn't complain about the way the world was going, as far back as Plato. Complaints about young people as if every generation of adults didn't complain about the young, as far back as Aristotle. Complaints about everything changing as if somehow you can stop the world going round so that those who don't want to change can get off at the next bus stop.

You know we're so good at lamenting things that some of us have made lamenting our lives work. If we could lament for Ireland in the Olympics we'd win gold, silver and bronze. And you know so much of that lamenting when you examine it, is plain and simple ingratitude.

Let me give you an example. I knew a man once who didn't like all the changes that were taking place in the world so he decided that he wouldn't go along with them. So he wouldn't let the electricity into the house. There was no running water in the house even though it was going past his front door. There was a well at the end of the field, and it did his father before him and his father before him again and it would do him while he was in it. So his wife – not him, mind you – but his wife spent a lifetime carrying buckets of water from the well at the end of a field.

In the world they lived in that was the way it was. He made the decision and she bore the brunt of it. Now if something like that happened today a wife would put down her foot and tell him to cop himself on because that's the way it is today and thank God for it.

And thank God for the changes that have helped to make life fuller and richer and happier than it was. Thank God for the running water, and the electricity and the fridge and the cooker and the heating and the hoover and all the things that have helped take the drudgery out of life. And thank God for the tractor and the milking machine and the Marts and the technology that have improved the working lives of so many people. And thank God for the ease of travel that allows people to come home at Christmas or to fly into Knock to attend a funeral at short notice.

Thank God for the television in the corner and the number of channels we can flick over and back to and for the good homes so many have and the few pounds in our pockets. And thank God for all the changes that have taken place that have enriched the life of our people. And, you know, the good old days, when you put them under a microscope, weren't as good as we sometimes imagine they were, when we begin to reminisce or we happen to have a few drinks taken. Nostalgia has a way of leaving out the bad times when we reminisce about the good old days. These are the good times. We're living through them now and the first thing we should do is thank God for them.

Imagine the age of the world is the equivalent of a rope four hundred-metres long. 99.9 per cent of the technological development in the history of the world has taken place in the last two centimetres of that rope. And we were here to witness it and to benefit from it. What a privilege that was, what a privilege it is to be alive at this extraordinary time. So instead of lamenting the state of the world, we should be on our knees thanking God for his goodness to us and joyfully living to the fullest every second that God gives us.

But the tragedy is that so often so many of us, like the man with the piped water running outside his door, instead of thanking God for everything he's given us, we're throwing God's gifts back in his face.

So let's thank God, for Mayo walking out on Croke Park tomorrow, for this moment in time, for the hope it inspires in us, for the joy it gives so many people, for the happiness it has brought and for the sense of energy and life it has given to so many people. 'I have come,' Jesus said, 'so that you may have life and live it to the full.' And at the end of the day, that's what religion is about: gratitude and joy.

A PRODIGAL GOD
The fondness of God

Many years ago David Frost was interviewing the late Cardinal Heenan of Westminster on television and he asked the Cardinal what part of the gospel he found it most difficult to accept. The Cardinal thought for a moment and then said that the part of the gospel he found it most difficult to accept was that God loved him as he was.

I think most of us, if we think about it, would agree with that. We have no problem believing that God loves us when we're good. We find it difficult to believe that God loves us even when we sin.

And the reason is, of course, that, in life, so much of our experience of love is that love is conditional. I'll love you if. I'll love you if you'll do this or say that or give me something or if you're faithful or whatever.

So much of love is conditional that we find it difficult to imagine that anyone could actually love us just as we are. And some of us, because of the way we were reared or the sermons we had to listen to or the attitudes we picked up from those around us, some of us would find it particularly difficult to imagine that God loved us just as we are and that nothing we would ever do would lessen the love God has for us.

So we saw God as a judge waiting to hand down the appropriate sentence on the last day. Or God was a teacher checking us at every turn and marking our lives as if they were an examination paper. Or God was a huge computer in the sky with a vast memory bank storing up the sins and failings of the human race. Or God, as Nancy Griffith says in her famous song, God is watching us all the time and everywhere.

But when we read about the God of the gospels, when we look at what Jesus did and said, we find a completely different God. Not a God who says 'I'll love you if . . .' but a kind and caring and compassionate and loving God who says to us 'I'll love you regardless.'

An American priest, a few years ago, was on a walking tour of Ireland, and one day he took shelter from the rain and he struck up a conversation with an old man and for some reason the conversation turned to prayer. The old man told the priest that he often had conversations with God, and he found it easy to talk to God because, he said, 'You know God is very fond of me.'

If I had a magic wand today, if I had a wish on this day that I would want to come true, my wish would be that every single one of us in this church would experience what that old man had obviously experienced, the *fondness* of God – the belief, the knowledge that God is very fond of us.

We didn't hear that at the missions long ago when the missioners were ranting about sin, and some of us didn't hear it in school or at home. What we heard about was a great accountant in the sky, watching us from a distance and checking our sins and indiscretions. So loving that great accountant became a long, convoluted process of fulfiling obligations, or doing things out of fear, or building up graces like a pension scheme. Instead of recognising that the God of the Gospels is someone who is fond of us, someone who loves us just as we are.

I remember meeting a woman one time who lost her daughter in tragic circumstances. She was a very religious woman and like the old man I mentioned earlier she didn't so much say her prayers as, she said herself, she had her chats with God. And the death of her daughter was a terrible cross for her and I remember her saying to me one day, 'I've been scolding God about what happened to Teresa.' *Scolding* like *fondness* are very Irish words that have to do with a great closeness and that experience of closeness is what the God of the gospels calls us into. God is fond of us, God is close to us, God loves us regardless of who we are or what we've done.

And the great problem for us understanding and accepting that, is that it doesn't fit in with our human experience. If you take forgiveness, for example. If someone offends us, often a precondition of our forgiveness is that some restitution is made.

An apology is sought or some condition has to be fulfiled almost like a fine having to be paid. Forgiveness, at the human level, in some sense has to be earned.

But God's forgiveness is completely different. It doesn't come out of an attitude that says, 'I'll forgive you if . . .' It says, 'I'll forgive you regardless . . .'

With people you have to be sorry first and then you earn their forgiveness. But with the God of the gospels, with the God of Jesus Christ, you know you'll be forgiven and through the experience of forgiveness a real sense of sorrow emerges. The message is that God is very fond of us and that God's forgiveness is available to everyone, all the time. It was available to the Prodigal Son as the Father waited for his son to come home, and then ran out to meet him and welcome him back. It was available to the paralytic in the gospel and it's available all the time and everywhere to me and to you.

FAITH
Fishermen in sailing boats

BOTTLED water is, I think an apt symbol of progress in Ireland today. Can you imagine what they'd have said fifty years ago if someone told them that we'd be paying £1 a bottle for water in the shops? Yet now we take it for granted. It's just part of the progress or at least the change that we don't notice anymore.

And side by side with change has come a loss of faith. The more self-sufficient we get, the less room there seems to be for God. There was a time when we used to pray for fine weather - now we look at the weather forecast.

There's a saying: Fishermen in sailing boats believe in God more easily than fishermen in motor-boats. What has happened is that in our lives the space that God used to fill and used to influence is getting smaller and smaller as science and technology become more important.

So faith in God is under pressure because of technology and change. Another reason why faith is under pressure is that until recently faith used to have the strong support of family, school and of place. I'm not saying that faith was easy in the past - far from it - but the very texture of life in the past was shot through with a sense of God and of religious faith.

Practically everybody went to Mass. Saying your prayers was part and parcel of life. It was second nature to bless ourselves going past a church or a graveyard. God and the things of God were part and parcel of the way we lived.

I was watching Kevin Keegan on television recently - he was the manager of the English soccer team - and he was being interviewed about it. And I noticed he kept saying things like 'with God's help' and 'please God.' It's very unusual now to hear a public figure in England or in Ireland speak like that anymore and yet just a few years ago practically everyone spoke like that.

So even the way we speak has changed and that's part of a change in our lifestyle and the gap that's emerging between, on the one hand, the preoccupations and the pressures of modern life and, on the other hand, what our faith tells us.

An example of this change in our lifestyles is that there are now fewer sacred times and sacred places in our lives. We're busy. We're preoccupied with work. We have to have a wonderful time, when we're not working. We have to have our time off. We have to drink so many pints every weekend. We have to get to that disco. We have to have this, that and the other. And what happens is that we find ourselves on a thread-mill of work and study and exams and discos and getting on and having boyfriends and girlfriends and getting married and getting a house and trying to pay the mortgage and trying to keep the money coming in and having a family. And finding too that we seem to be having less and less space for God, finding that we have fewer and fewer sacred times and sacred places in our lives.

And then at particular times in our lives, we can get a sense of how shallow so much of our lives have become.

A baby is born and the extraordinary miracle of birth stops us in our tracks. Or someone we love is dying and there's nothing we can do but leave him or her in the hands of God. And we begin to get a sense of how in comparison to birth or death or contentment or happiness, how futile and empty is so much of what we we think is important.

I'm not saying that progress and money and making a good living and having a nice home and wanting to be self-fulfiled and happy, I'm not saying that there's anything wrong with all of of that. Far from it. We were long enough poverty-stricken and there wasn't much joy in it.

But what I am saying is that if in the new culture that is emerging in Ireland all we have is money and what money can buy, we'll end up as the poorest of the poor. If in the culture that's emerging in Ireland, if there isn't place and space for wonder and for mystery and for God, then all the money and property and influence and anything else will ultimately be like so much sand running through our fingers.

If I haven't in my life a sense of awe, a sense of wonder, a sense of God. If I haven't in my life a sense that above and beyond and outside what I can see and feel and possess, a sense that there is another wisdom that gives substance to the life I'm living, then I will have lost something very precious indeed.

And this is where we are now facing as a society. We can use out time and our energy squeezing out of life every last pound or euro. We can run ourselves into the ground getting our hands on every possession we can possibly get. We can focus every ounce of energy into making a career for ourselves but if we lose our sense of wonder then no matter what we have we'll be the poorest of the poor.

I sometimes watch my little grandnephews and grandnieces - they're just two and four and six, round that age - and I often wonder what life will be like for them. It's a hard world they're facing into, but it's a world too in many ways that has more going for it, than in their fathers and grandfathers day. I hope that they'll have good lives, that they'll get satisfying work, that they'll make good relationships, that they'll be blessed with good health. And I hope that, all things considered, I hope that they'll live happy and contented lives.

That's a lot to hope for. But even if they get all of that, there's something more important than all of that that I wish for them. I would want them to have a sense of awe, a sense of wonder, a sense of mystery and, above all, a sense of God. Because I believe that faith, that wonder, that sense of something more that that would give them a depth and a richness that nothing else in life could possibly give them. I would want them to understand and to experience the jewel of faith that came down through the generations before us, that sense of God and the things of God that passed through so many lives and so many families and so many parishes and so many faith-communities and that they too one day would want to pass on that jewel to their own children and to their children's children.

We have to keep reminding ourselves that at the heart of life there is a wisdom and a richness that comes from having a sense of awe, a sense of wonder, a sense that above and beyond and outside this present life there is a reality that gives depth and richness and substance to the lives that we lead on this day.

SIN
The God I believe in

Igrew up in a place called Ballycastle, in Co Mayo. Growing up in the Fifties in Ballycastle was, I'm sure, a bit like growing up anywhere in the Fifties. Times were hard, resources were minimal, it was a dull and uninteresting time. As I remember it, the most exciting thing that happened on a Sunday evening in Ballycastle in the Fifties was Rosary and Benediction. Rural Ireland in the Fifties hadn't a lot going for it at the time. But that was the way it was and looking back one of the things that strikes me is how good we were as young kids.

Apart from the usual scrapes that kids get involved in the only thing I remember doing out of the way was stealing apples from the parish priest's orchard. The parish priest in question was the late Canon Maloney and of course the fact that they were the Parish Priest's apples added an extra bit of excitement to the whole enterprise.

At the time we took it in our stride. But the following year I went to boarding school and during first year at boarding school we had a retreat. And the retreat master gave a talk about hell and eternity.

I can remember distinctly to this day every word he said. He described eternity for us. Imagine, he said, a seagull at the sea, and in coming in to land the wing of the seagull brushes against a huge rock. And how many seagulls, he asked rhetorically, will have to brush against that rock with their wings for that rock to be completely worn away. How long will it take?

And he paused to let the enormity of it sink in and then he said, very solemnly: 'The length it will take,' he said, 'is only a fraction of the length of eternity.' And then he went on to describe the fires of hell in graphic detail and he ended with his punch-line: 'If you die in the state of mortal sin you will suffer in Hell for all eternity.'

The result, of course, was that he frightened the daylights out of us. I don't know what the other lads saw, but I saw the apples in Canon Maloney's garden and there was a long queue for Confessions that evening.

I remember going to Confession and telling my big sin and the priest was very kind and I remember him telling how wrong it was to take something that didn't belong to you. That's what he was trying to get across but what was left with me was the fact that I could have suffered the fires of Hell for all eternity for stealing a few lousy apples from Canon Maloney's Garden.

It took me a long time to get over that because what was implanted in my mind as a child was that the God I prayed to was a God who would condemn me to that eternal punishment for stealing a few apples and that if I was to get to Heaven one day it would depend on my ability to avoid sin.

And of course not only is that untrue. It's actually heresy. It's something that as followers of Jesus Christ, it's something that as a Church we simply do not believe.

We won't get to Heaven because we've earned it. We'll get to Heaven because God loves us so much that every sin we have committed and every sin we will ever commit have already been forgiven through the coming of his Son into the world and through the life he lived and the death he experienced. That's God's gift to us, and everything that flows from it is God's gift to us. Nobody in this church will get to heaven because he or she deserves it. We won't get to heaven because we've gone to Mass every Sunday or because we've never missed our morning prayers or because we've done this or that Novena. We'll get to Heaven because God loves us so much that he will gift us with the happiness of Heaven.

I find that when I say this to people they sometimes react by saying: 'But doesn't that mean so that you can commit any sin you want and you'll get to heaven anyway. So why bother to live a good life?' (That's a bit like the priest who was asked by a class of teenagers: 'Was sex before marriage a sin?' and his reply was, 'Sure, of course, it's a sin wouldn't we be all at it if it wasn't?')

And that's the key point: What is sin? And a simple definition of sin is this: sin is turning away from God, sin is not loving God. But just as you can only know what a straight line is, if you first know what a crooked line is, you can only know what it is *not to love God* if you know what it is to *love God* and have had some sense of being loved by God.

What kind of relationship would you have with a parent whom you visited out of a sense of obligation and not out of love? What kind of relationship would you have with your wife or your husband if you were to say I'm going to remain faithful to you because it's a sin not to!

But, you see, the tragedy is that so many people are stuck in this understanding of religion that if I don't do this or if I don't avoid that that God will not love me and God will punish me for it, possibly by sending me to Hell for all eternity. Again, let me say, that that's heresy.

We believe that there is no limit to God's love. We believe that there is no point at which God says this far and no further. And we believe that there is no sense in which God's love is earned by what we do or what we don't do.

God loves us. Full stop. That's our faith. But unfortunately that's not what many of us actually believe. Isn't it so sad to meet good and decent people who have lived good and decent lives and they committed a few sins in their youth and they've spent a lifetime picking over them, confessing them over and over again as if somehow God couldn't possibly have forgiven them. Or good and honest and decent people who have said their prayers and gone to Mass and lived good and decent and loving lives, and they come to the end of their days worrying about sins they mightn't have confessed or sins they might have forgotten and they imagine that loving God is a bit like that game we used to play years ago as children, *Snakes and Ladders.*

Do you remember it? You went up the ladder if you got a break but as sure as night followed day there was a snake around the corner and you went sliding down again. You went to Confession and you sped up the ladder. Then you committed a sin and you slid down the snake. And more often than not you were left with the image of a God who was trying to catch you out, trying to get some excuse *not* to let you into heaven.

Let me spell it out very clearly what we believe about God. We believe that God loved us so much that he sent his Son into this world to die for our sins.

And he died for every sin any of us has committed, and he died for every sin we have yet to commit. That's what we mean when we say that we are a redeemed people. We have been redeemed through the death of Christ and out of the love that God has for us we are called to love him in return and to love one another.

But the Christian religion is not just about loving God and loving one another. That's part of it and that part is what the commandments tell us in the Old Testament. But what Jesus said to us in the New Testament was, 'Love one another, as I have loved you.' He also said, 'I have come that you may have life and live it to the full.' So the God we believe in is a God who loves us with a love beyond human understanding.

The parable of the sower and the seed makes the point that despite the ups and downs of life, God is with us, God has pitched his tent among us. So the parable of the sower and the seed is a parable of encouragement. It's saying to us. 'Don't be discouraged because God is with us. It isn't just the sower and the seed that are important. It's God who ultimately produces the harvest.'

Let me end with this quotation from the late Cardinal Basil Hume. For obvious reasons it meant a lot to me. It might mean something to you too. This is what he wrote, *'I remember something I was told when I was a very small boy. In the larder there was a stock of apples. A small boy wanted an apple. He had been told by some grown-up that he must not take things without permission. But why not take just one, he thought! Nobody would know. It just seemed common sense. Nobody would see him. Was that true? Nobody? One person would. That was God. He sees everything you do, and then punishes you for wrongdoing. So I was told. It took me many years to recover from that story. Deep in my subconscious was the idea of God as somebody who was always watching us just to see if we were doing anything wrong. He was an authority figure, like a teacher or a policeman or even a bishop.*

Now many years later, I have an idea that God would have said to the small boy 'Take two apples.' I agree with that.

THE MARGINS
Drawing the line

THE days we spent at school have left their own distinctive impressions. Even as far back as the early days in school, the days when we made our first crooked letters and figures. And the days too when our first teacher showed us how to rule our copies - leaving a margin on the side of the page where we could do the rough work and keeping the rest of the page for the really important sums. With a bit of practice it became second nature for us to make a margin on the page, to draw a line between what was important, special, acceptable and what could be relegated to the margin.

Maybe, in a sense, it became a bit too easy for us to make the margin, to draw the line. Because for many of us, it has become second nature to draw the line, not just on the page, not just when it has to do with copy books and sums, but when it has to do with people.

The world we live in is a world where the centre of the page is given to some people and the rest are confined to the margin. If you have money or power or influence people instinctively move you into the centre of the page. If you don't fit into what our society determines success to be, you find yourself on the margins.

Of course we're not the only generation ever to do this. It has always been done even as far back as the time of Leviticus when we're told that 'the leper had to live apart, he had to live outside the camp.' Because for Leviticus the leper was a marginal person, someone to be kept on the sideline, someone to be kept out of sight and out of mind. We would now react against that kind of distinction. We would see it as anti-social, barbaric, uncivilised and especially as unChristian. Leprosy was a terrible disease and apparently it still exists but we don't reject lepers now as 'unclean.' We see them as people with a disease that needs to be cured. We see them as individual people who deserve our help and our respect.

We've come a long way since the time of Leviticus, and yet who could say that in the society we live in today that a form of leprosy doesn't exist? Who could say that we're not still drawing the line on the page of life and relegating people to the margins? I think of people who have Aids, those who have it and those afraid to admit that they have it - individuals and families caught in a life-threatening and respect-threatening bind that eats away at their dignity and self-respect. I think of people who have abused children and the limited existence they have and how easy it is for society to push them to the outer margins. I think of Traveller families living in appaling conditions on the side of the road. For example, a family of nine children at the moment, living in a caravan with no water, no electric power, no sanitary facilities and the money to build them a home is lying for years in a bank account in Dublin and can't be used because people who are at Mass today object to them living near them. I think of children born with no hope of a future in this rich and successful country. I think of how the governor of Mountjoy Jail, John Lonergan, recently said that if he walked through the wards of the great maternity hospitals in Dublin he could predict, almost to the last cot, from the areas in Dublin those babies will grow up which of them will end up, in Mountjoy in 16 or 17 or 25 years time.

So every society and indeed every generation draws a line on the page of life, between acceptability and non-acceptability, between respectability and non-respectability and that line can shift and change from generation to generation.

There was a time, for example, when children with a mental handicap were treated with less than adequate respect and that attitude changed because people worked at changing it. There was a time when our attitude to one-parent families was hostile and condemnatory and now in a different world it's accepted that the definition of family has been respectfully widened. And the opposite is true too. There was a time, for example, when we were noted as a country for our care of the elderly, but I don't

know if that's still as true as it was. So we still have our
marginal people, and we still have this tendency to draw a line
on a page.

The response of Jesus to the leper, the outcast was to take the
leper out of the margin of life and to bring him into the centre of
the page. And the result of it all, we're told in the gospel, is that
the leper went off and told everyone what Jesus had done for
him, and Jesus to avoid the crowd, had 'to stay outside in places
where nobody lived'. Jesus had to confine himself to the margin.
And that's sometimes what happens when we do what Jesus
asks us to do. What happens is that we too can find ourselves
being pushed to the margins. And that's not a bad place for
anyone who genuinely wants to follow the way of Jesus.

Because Jesus himself was a marginal person, he died
despised and rejected, nailed by society to a cross between two
thieves. So as his followers I think we should be doing two
things: we should be drawing people who are on the margins,
back into the centre of life. And for those who are not allowed
into the centre, we should be happy to stay with them on the
margins.

So Jesus calls us not to sit in judgement on our fellow human
beings, but to treat every person with respect and to treat them
with dignity, no matter who they are, or where they live, or what
they've going for them or against them. Every person is made in
God's image and every person deserves respect. So we should be
careful - those of us who profess to be his followers - not to be
tempted to push people to the margins of life. At the very core of
our faith, is an acceptance of every human person and that isn't
just the kind of vague uninvolved tolerance we find in modern
life today. A truly Christian acceptance of every individual person
is about drawing people from the margins and about going to the
margins to be in solidarity with those who are not allowed into
the centre.

LISTENING
Hearing the right voices

THE old cliche is that when God made us, he gave us two ears and one mouth, and that in so doing God was trying to tell us that we should listen twice as much as we should speak. We don't do that, of course. Most people are either bad listeners or very bad listeners or terrible listeners. Even people who imagine they're good listeners are often bad listeners.

Usually most of us have plenty to say, usually most of us enjoy saying it, and usually most of don't want to listen to what others have to say. We may be present to people; we may even be looking at people directly; we may be saying nothing; we may even be nodding our heads but that doesn't mean that we actually hear what's they're saying.

And yet listening is one of the most important things in life. And the reason is that if there's no listening, there's no communication. And good communication is vital in every walk of life and in every relationship. And if there's no real listening, then, as we all know, there are real problems.

We see it in the blood transfusion controversy when it took the death of a woman to make the authorities actually hear what was being said. We saw it in the reaction of Church authorities when the sexual abuse of children by clergy was revealed first - the terrible failure there was to hear the pain of individuals and families. And we see it all around us in the devastation that's caused in relationships when people speak and they know they're not being heard.

Listening is a skill and a discipline. It's something that we have to force ourselves to learn to do because the prevailing culture we live in is running directly opposed to it. Our culture is talk, talk and endless talk and most of the time most of the listeners aren't hearing a word of what's being said. We often talk past each other.

Part of the problem is how busy everyone seems to be. We never had more time-saving equipment in our homes, at our work, in the way we travel, and so on. And yet we're all spending our lives running around trying to keep up with ourselves. We haven't time for a proper conversation; we haven't time to sit down and enjoy our meals; we haven't time almost to bid each other the time of day. So we live out lives in a rush. The children have their homework to do and their karate classes and football and gymnastics and . . . Parents have to go to work and do the shopping and clean the house and go out on the weekend and there's no time for listening because listening eats up time.

Listening needs time and space and silence, the very things we don't seem to have anymore. Isn't it extraordinary that when people fall in love, they want to spend time together; they want to stay out until 6 o'clock in the morning discussing every subject under the sun; they want to talk and talk and talk and listen and listen and listen; and they want to invest time in getting to know each other. And then they get married and they have children and there's so much to do that they end up having no time for themselves, even not talking that much to one another and sometimes not listening at all. And gradually the distance between them widens and they often end up going to other people saying the things that their own spouse needs to hear but won't take the time to hear . . .

Is there anything sadder in life than a wife or a husband having to say to a complete stranger what they want to say to their own spouse. And what's the greatest regret that spouses and parents have on their death bed? More often than not it's that they didn't invest more time in each other and in their children. It's practically a universal experience but how many learn from it? I think too the fact that we are a non-listening generation has something to do with the fact that we've become a less believing generation. Because religion, faith, the God-thing as it's sometimes described, can't be rushed. We can no more rush ourselves into belief or presume belief than we can rush children into Mass and presume that they'll want to go for the rest of their lives.

Religion isn't like that. Making contact with a personal God isn't something you can rush like filling out a form. It needs space and time and above all it needs the ability to listen, to listen to God and to listen to those who can put us in touch with God. Because the call of God will only be heard if we create the circumstances that will allow it to be heard.

When God called Samuel, he called him three times and even then Eli had to tell him that it was the Lord calling him. And in the gospel it was John the Baptist who had to point out Jesus to the disciples before Jesus called out to them "Come and see"

We find God or rather maybe God finds us above all in solitude and in silence in the reflective and quiet mood that allows us to say with Samuel 'Speak, Lord, your servant is listening.' But today we're often uncomfortable with silence and many of us can't take solitude at all. And yet how can we possibly make contact with God or allow God to make contact with us unless we have in our lives some oasis of silence and solitude that will help us to hear the call of God in our busy, busy lives.

If you're in business today, you're going to be tempted to cut corners, to make a fast pound by bending the rules, and so many today say, 'Well, that's business.' But when you're tempted to do that there will be a small and a still voice telling you that what you're doing is wrong. But if in your busy, busy life if there's no oasis of silence and solitude then the call of God – because that's what the small and still voice is – then the call of God will not be heard. If you're a married person today you're going to be tempted to be unfaithful, and you'll have plenty of opportunity to be unfaithful, and when the possibility for that comes there will a small and a still voice telling you that what you're doing is wrong. But if in your married life if there's no oasis of silence and solitude then the call of God – because that's what that small and still voice is – will not be heard.

If you're a young person today you're going to be tempted to take drugs, to abuse alcohol, to be sexually active, and when the possibility for all of that or some of that arises, there will a small and a still voice telling you that what you're doing is wrong. But if there's no oasis of silence and solitude then the call of God, because that's what that small and still voice is, then the call of God will not be heard.

You see it's not that God isn't speaking to us, it's not that God isn't knocking on the door of our hearts. It's simply that we've allowed life and time and space to become cluttered up with work and recreation and noise and people. It's because we have no listening centre in our lives, no space, no solitude, no silence, that we've succeeded in blotting out the very voices we need to hear for love and for happiness in our lives.

An old priest said to me once, 'If you're too busy to pray, then you're too busy.' And I think that we can widen that to include all the really important areas of our lives. If we're too busy to give time and space to what really matters then we're too busy. If we haven't a place of silence and solitude in our lives to allow us to hear the voices that really matter, then we can have everything going for us, we can be a success in every way success is measured in the world, but at the end of the day, we'll have nothing to show for it.

Because ultimately all that matters in life is being able to hear the right voices.

MOTHER'S DAY
An uncompromising love

BIRTHDAYS are important occasions. They help us to take stock of ourselves, to have a look at *who* we are and *what* we are and *where* we are. Great feast-days like Christmas and Easter are the same. Like birthdays they give us an excuse for celebrating and they help us to take stock of *what* we are and *where* we are as a people. And days like Mother's Day are the same. They help us take stock of *who* we are and more importantly *who* has made us *what* we are. They give us too a sense of a clock ticking away, of the fact that there will be come a day when we won't be able to send a Mother's Day card or say thanks to our mothers for a love beyond caring.

Days like Mother's Day too are a time for reflecting: on what mothers are, on what mothers do, and, in a more personal sense, on the company or memory of our own mothers. So today on Mother's Day, our thoughts are with all mothers, living and dead. This Mother's Day, for me, is different from any other I have ever known. For me, and for those of us who have lost our mothers during the course of the year, this Mother's Day has its own bitter-sweet character.

It's a cliche to say that you never miss the water until the well runs dry and we never really miss those close to us, until we actually experience what their absence feels like, until we feel the texture of that absence.

That's true, I believe, of husbands and wives who lose their spouses. That's true, I believe, of parents who lose their children. And that's true, I know, of children who lose their parents.

In a sense, no matter how old we are, we remain children while our parents are alive. We remain children in our parents' eyes and, to some degree at least, in our own eyes.

When we have parents with us, we have no experience of life without them, and, in our childish eyes, there seems to be almost an air of indestructibility about them.

My own mother, God rest her, died before Christmas. I never, ever remember her being a day sick in her life so there was that sense that other people would lose their mothers but that I would never lose mine. I think there's something of that in a lot of us. We can't envisage life without them, because we have known no other, and because we can't envisage life without them, we imagine it will never be real for us.

Another thing is that when we lose a mother or a father, in most cases at least, we lose the experience of someone who loved us unconditionally, someone who loved us not because of what we've achieved or how important we are or what we can give but simply because of who we are. And that, in a sense, for those of us who have lost our mothers, that is part of what we miss on Mother's Day, that experience of uncompromising love that knew no limits. I remember one time seeing an interview on television with the mother of Thomas Hamilton, the man who shot dead the innocent children of Dunblane. And there she was, the poor woman, trying to defend her son, possibly the only person in the world who had a good word to say for him. She was like all mothers, a mother to the end. It's that uncompromising and unqualified love that we celebrate on Mother's Day

The older I get, and the fewer the bits of wisdom I have, I remain convinced of this: that bringing a child into the world seems, in some respects, like the beginning a life sentence. Because children in a strange way become the agents of their parents' happiness. Today all over Ireland there will be mothers whose heart will be lifted by a little card scribbled in school in a shaky hand that says, 'To the best Mum in the World.' And tomorrow too all over Ireland there will be mothers too, who will need some equivalent of that little card, some indication that the love that they hold in their hearts will be reciprocated in some symbolic way, through a card or a box of chocolates or whatever. And, we know too, don't we, that today all over Ireland, there will be mothers who will watch the door in vain waiting for a visit from their child and mothers who wait for the phone to ring just to hear their child say 'Happy Mother's Day.' And like

Christmas some will come and some won't come; some will ring; and some won't bother to ring. And some mothers will, like in the dark days after Christmas, some mothers will sit in the shadows in lonely rooms and they will try to rationalise their children's neglect and they'll even blame themselves that they didn't rear them properly. And they will shed their own private tears because all they wanted was some gesture, some indication that the love and the sacrifice was noticed, some sense that there was some memory of the nights when we were sick and our mothers sat up with us all night, some memory of the time and the effort and the money they spent on us that they could have spent on themselves, just some indication that all that love that we talk about when our mothers are dead, that all that love mattered before they died.

So if you're lucky enough to have mother with you, then mark Mother's Day today. Buy your mother a box of chocolates or give her a card that she can put up on the mantelpiece and go to see her today and if you can't give her a ring. I know and you know what mothers say: 'Amen't I alright', 'Sure I don't need anything', 'You've little enough for yourself.' And they'll pretend that they don't need you to mark Mother's Day for them. But they do because in the dusk of a winter's evening these are the things that they remember: that indication of love; that sense that all the sacrifices are at least acknowledged, if not reciprocated; that warm feeling that the love that burned in their hearts for all of us, has found an echo in our gratitude. And if your Mother is still with you, and if she won't hear tell of you marking Mother's Day for her, let me give you a bit of advice that I wasn't in a position to give last year: if she won't let you do it for her, then do it for yourself. It's something that if our mothers don't want us to do for them, we need to do for ourselves. And finally we think of all mothers who have died and we remember to pray for them on Mother's Day and maybe visit their graves. And a memory too for mothers unknown, for the mothers who, died before their children were old enough to really get to know them, for the natural mothers of adopted children who in whatever circumstances, had to give up their children for adoption and for adoptive mothers who gave and continue to give such unselfish love to their adopted children. May God be with you and with yours wherever they may be this Mother's Day.

GRATITUDE
The important ingredient

JUST suppose that God gave each of us a copy-book and told us to write two things: the names of the people who mean most to us in life and the things we would most like them to have. What would you write?

If you were God for a moment, what would you give your spouse, your children, your parents, the person you love? Think about it. Or maybe you wouldn't even have to think about it.

That right examination result in the Leaving Cert? That job? That life? That house? Winning the Lotto tonight? Or whatever? Obviously, it would be something that would contribute to their happiness but that brings up the difficult question about what happiness is?

I don't know what the magic ingredient for lifelong happiness is. I don't know the great secret of life but as far as I can see the people who come closest to finding it are those whose response to the life God has given them is an overwhelming sense of gratitude. And it's not just a sense of gratitude as we understand it. It's wider and deeper and richer than that. It's a sense of appreciation. It's ultimately a sense of acceptance. It's a way of looking at the world and human kind and our own lives and being able to appreciate the good things we have, to be able to see, even in the most difficult of situations, the giftedness of the lives we lead.

The holiest people in the world are not those who go to Mass every day, or those who say hundreds of prayers or those who perform religious exercises to the last detail. The holiest people in the world are those who can link into the giftedness that has come from God into their lives.

The problem with the rest of us is that humanly speaking it's almost impossible to appreciate something if you have no experience of not having it. People who were never sick a day in their lives tend not to appreciate the gift of health because they have never had the experience of ill-health. People who have always had the gift of sight don't really experience, in a sense, can't really experience, what it is is to be blind.

With the result that we tend to take for granted what we have and often spend much of our lives searching for and wanting what we haven't got. The hills far away are always that much greener. It's always easier to do the washing-up in someone else's house. But here and there we can get a glimpse of that magic ingredient, that element that contributes to our personal happiness: in the old person who can thank God for every day that comes rather than becoming moody and irritable with the stresses of old age; in the farmer who can accept the rainy day rather than becoming depressed and upset; in the Massgoer who feels it a privilege and an opportunity to share in the Mass and to receive the Bread of Life at God's altar rather than those who complain if it goes on five minutes longer than usual. In such people there is a sense of gratitude, a sense of appreciation of the giftedness of God.

The opposite of gratitude is not so much ingratitude as regret and regret is probably one of the most destructive features of life. Most of us wouldn't go so far as Woody Allen who said once that his only regret in life was that he wasn't someone else but regret can so easily dominate our thoughts. Instead of joyfully accepting and using and thanking God for the gifts he has given us, we begin to regret not having this or that particular gift, not being in this or that particular situation. From that regret we can build a great house of envy and jealousy and sometimes we're not even content with that unless we build on rooms of bitterness and self-pity and all we're doing is carving out a great deal of unhappiness for ourselves.

God has given you and given me all that you and I need to be happy. God has given you and me all the gifts we need in life. The problem is not that God's plans have gone wrong somewhere along the line, the problem is with you and me and with our attitude to what God has given us.

So instead of pining for the things that God in his wisdom

decided we shouldn't have, we should thank God for his goodness in giving us what we need.

For the health of mind and body that are so precious; for the children growing up in the homes of our parish; for the work we do; for the recreation we enjoy; for the fresh air that we breathe; for the companionship and loyalty and love of those closest to us; for the friendship of our neighbours; for the sacrifices that parents make for their children; for the rich and deep faith that is obvious in the lives of so many of our people; for the grandeur and beauty of God's creation; for the variety and multiplicity of God's gifts.

So in this Mass, as we thank God for the gift of himself in the Eucharist, let us pray for a deep and abiding gratitude in our own lives and in the lives of those precious to us. That we may understand something of the graciousness and the giftedness of God and that we may come to appreciate a little bit more that goodness and that graciousness.

So that when we come to ponder what it is that we would most want those we love to have, we will be able to see the focus of that happiness not in something God may one day give us but in something that God has already given to us.

GETTING OUR ATTENTION
The grace of restlessness

ONE of the more obvious features of modern living is how restless we often are. We often feel that we should be more content than we are. We tell ourselves that we've a lot going for us. We can point to a number of reasons why we should be happy and fulfiled and content and yet sometimes we find ourselves asking the questions that sooner or late surface in every life: what's it all about? what's it all for? why am I not happier than I am?

Sometimes of course we don't allow the questions to surface. We deny the questions. We won't let our minds put words on them. Or we bury them beneath the compulsions of our lives. Or we kid ourselves into believing that we haven't the time or the space to deal with the questions that are always there just under the surface of our lives. And the more we bury the questions, the more desperate sometimes the denying seems to get.

So we distract ourselves. We have to get a bigger farm; we have to make the business even more successful; we have to have a better house; we have to have a more expensive holiday; we have to have the very latest in fashion; we have to have our football or our golf or our drinks; we have to have flat tummies; and we have to fill the quiet moments of our lives with noise and activity. And then suddenly in the middle of whatever project we happen to be involved with, a small voice insists on asking the questions we don't want to hear: what's it all for? what's it all about? why am I not happier than I am?

But even if we don't allow ourselves to ask the questions, it's only a temporary denial. Because somewhere in life, those questions are waiting for us to ambush us at some crossroads, to creep up on us unawares at one of the great intersections of life.

You sit in a hospital corridor and your father is dying a few feet away from you but you've got nothing to say to him. Your child is dying and you want to pray to God about it but you don't know the language anymore. Or you find yourself in some other situation and the elements of the life you have carefully constructed are falling down around you and you don't even care anymore. And sometimes, as a result, people break down in some way or get depressed or worried in case there isn't a God or sometimes worry in case there is a God or contemplate suicide or wonder how they're going to cope - anything just to quell the desperate restlessness of their lives.

There was a time when we knew what we wanted and we spent every ounce of energy we had trying to get it. And there was a time when we felt we had achieved what we had set our hearts on. And we got a certain satisfaction and fulfilment out of it. And then suddenly for no reason we got this feeling of vague dissatisfaction, a vague restlessness, and what we thought were important things didn't seem to matter that much anymore . . . and then we had to face the questions about who we are and what we are and what it all means.

And people found themselves saying, 'I have a job, I'm happily married, I have 2.5 children – or whatever the proper number is – I have a nice house,my children are healthy, life should be wonderful but why am I not happy?'

And if we're lucky we will sense that restlessness not as a disease that we have to inoculate ourselves against but as a grace that will help us get in touch with God. And if we're very lucky we'll create around us the time and the space to allow God to break into our world.

You know the old story of the carpenter and the apprentice. They were walking together through a great forest. And they came across a tall, huge, twisted, beautiful oak tree. And the carpenter turned to the apprentice and said:

Do you know why this tree is so tall and so huge and so twisted and so old and so beautiful? No, he said...why? Well, the carpenter replied, because it's useless. If it had been useful it would have been cut down long ago and made into chairs and tables, but because it is so useless it could grow so tall and so beautiful that you can sit in its shade and relax.

In other words there are some lessons that can only be learned in silence and in solitude. There are lessons that can only be learned if we can bear the silence long enough to hear God gently knocking on the door of our hearts. It's then that the great truth dawns on us, the truth that St Augustine summed up in the words, 'My heart is restless O God until it rests in you.'

So we need an antidote to the restlessness we often feel. We need something to help us to get our priorities in right order. And what we need is space and time to reflect on what really matters. The *Liveline* radio programme was recently discussing a growing problem today of people working too hard, working too long hours, and in the process sacrificing the things that really matter. Needing more and more money for a home and a family and spending so much time and effort and energy making more and more money that one day people suddenly wake up to discover that the home and the family and the marriage aren't there any more.

So we need to see these questions not as frightening us or dispiriting us but as God's way of getting our attention. It's God's way of asking us to be still, asking us to find a quiet space in our lives where we can stay with the questions, where we can face the pain that these questions inevitably surface. And the persistence of these questions, is the persistence of God continually knocking on the doors of our hearts down.

THINGS FALL APART
Hearing God's call

ONE of the prevailing moods of our time is a fear that somehow or other things are falling apart in our world. We live, of course, at a time of unprecedented change. Never in the history of humankind have things changed so much in such a short time. And change is difficult to cope with. Someone described living in the world as being like skiers in the middle of an avalanche, trying to hold our feet as the ground crumbles beneath us. And we think of the words of W.B. Yeats, 'Things fall apart, the centre cannot hold . . .'

There is a sense that the old world is crumbling and that no one is very sure what's going to emerge. We get the feeling sometimes that no one is in charge anymore, that anarchy prevails. So it may be important to get things into perspective. The answer to the question, 'Who is in charge of the world?' is the same answer as it ever was, 'God is in charge of the world.'

But people may say, 'Well, if He is, why are all these terrible things happening?' and the list is as long as a piece of string: the war in some foreign land, the abuse of children, domestic violence, the decline in respect, breakdown in different forms and so on.

And the simple answer is that terrible things are happening not because God wants them to happen. These awful things are happening because God has given human beings the freedom to make choices and when people make wrong choices then terrible things happen.

But even though human beings abuse the freedom God gives us, even though human beings have the capacity to bring untold hardship and misery to one another, we believe that God is the ultimate authority in our world and that the evil we are responsible for, in the wrong or bad or immoral decisions we make, that evil will never triumph over the good and the right and the true, that God represents. And that's a great consolation.

It's a consolation on a world scale that the evil of war will never triumph over the good and the God of peace; it's a consolation to know that at a community level, the forces of disunity and division and conflict will never ultimately triumph over those who work for unity and brotherhood and development; it's a consolation to know that your sins and my sins won't triumph over the good that God calls forth in each of us to overcome our failures and our limitations; and it's a consolation to know that a God of love and peace and mercy continues to hold the world and this community and your life and mine in the cradle of his hand.

And things go wrong for the world and for you and for me, because of the decisions we make - when we leave aside the good of peace and friendship for the bad of conflict and disruption, when we leave aside the freedom we have to choose what is good and right and true for the freedom to choose what is not right and not good and not true.

The God we believe in is a God of authority - the God who spoke through the prophets in the Old Testament, the God who spoke in the person of Jesus Christ in the New Testament, the God who still speaks to us century after century, year after year, need after need, through the Church he founded, that God still speaks to our world, to the community, and to you and to me. He's a God of authority - yes, but he's a God who has dignified us with the freedom to choose - to make our own choices, to make decisions. And he's a God who calls out to us, asking us to pay attention to the message he gives us, asking us in the words of the psalm not to harden our hearts but to open our hearts to the message of faith, hope and love, the message of forgiveness and reconciliation, the message of justice and truth that he offers to us.

And what our world becomes, what this community is, what you or I are like, depends on whether we hear the voice of God calling to us and how we respond to that voice.

THE OMAGHS OF OUR TIMES
Only God knows

URING the week I heard the mother of James Barker talk on radio. You may remember that James Barker was one of the Omagh victims, he was twelve years of age when he lost his life in the Omagh bombing. His mother never changed anything in his room; it's left exactly as it was; the bed made; the usual bits and pieces of a boy's life left around, the door constantly left open.

If there was no bomb in Omagh this day last year James would now be thirteen years of age.

If there was no bomb in Omagh this day last year, this week would have been just another ordinary week in the life of his mother. Instead she sits and looks into his room, a shrine to his memory, a shrine too to his mother's sorrow and her inability to deal with her grief.

And the pain of that mother is repeated in twenty-seven other homes and in hundreds and hundreds of other homes in the North of Ireland and beyond the north, a mountain of pain and distress, unimaginable to anyone except those who have gone through that Garden of Gethsemane. And in the context of that terrible distress and that unimaginable pain, everything else pales into insignificance. This time last year, the Leaving Certificate results, the great sports stories, and everything else played a supporting role in the media and in our lives, to the bombing of Omagh and the dreadful, unquantifiable fall-out from that outrage.

I say 'unquantifiable' because even though we can put numbers on the dead and injured, even though all the relevant statistics have all been set down, even though survivors and relatives have gone through trauma counselling and all the helps that are now available, the pain, the loss, the deprivation in its many and varied forms - that suffering is still there - and all of it is simply unquantifiable.

Because how can we quantify the loss of a twenty months old baby? Or a mother and her unborn twins? Or the violent and pointless loss of a wife or husband or a father or a mother? How can we quantify the loss of sight to a sixteen year-old girl or the loss of a limb? How can we quantify the psychological traumas that will for years obstruct the normality that is so precious in everyday living?

Only God knows where the fall-out from this bomb will eventually end. Only God knows where the ripples running out from the epicentre of this bomb will eventually reach. Only God knows, because in God's truth we certainly don't know. We can't see how anyone could possibly believe that such an act could achieve any benefit anytime anywhere. We can't see how such a devastating action can somehow be part of the tapestry of God's design for our world. We can't see at any level anything that makes sense in the mountain of pain and suffering that so many innocent people have so needlessly been asked to endure.

And because we can't see we can't find the words to make sense of it all. So all we can do is to acknowledge what has happened; all we can do is to name the truth as we see it; all we can do is to search our own consciences and to acknowledge in the deepest recesses of our own minds, to acknowledge and to own as individuals or as a nation, whatever personal or collective guilt may be there.

We may not have made or carried or driven or primed that bomb or any other bomb but all of that was done out of a tortured belief that death and destruction and violence and mayhem were acceptable and necessary strategies on the long road of Irish history that brought us finally to Omagh. So we look into our own hearts, examine our own consciences, pick out the half-truths that sought to defend the indefensible. Pick out too the half-hearted condemnations of other Omaghs and the convenient political posturings that refused to accept a clear difference between what's right and what's wrong.

We want to forget about Omagh; we want to move on to the rest of our lives; we want to push that eerie, split-second of silence before the screaming started in Omagh, captured so graphically on television out of sight and out of mind.

We thought, in our innocence, it was all over, that the last drop of blood had been shed, that the people had spoken in the two referenda, north and south.

The Good Friday Agreement was going to mean an end to it all. No more crosses to be carried, no more women of Jerusalem or of Belfast weeping for their children, no more northern Gethsemanes, no more Irish Calvarys.

It was a time of hope and promise. It was a new dawn after a long winter of despair. Songs of promise were sung; poems of a new day were written; words of hope were spoken.

So we pray for the dead of Omagh that they may be at peace. We pray for the injured, for all those whose lives are marred and disjointed or laid desolate. We ask God to give us the words so that even in the depths of distress and despair we might find a vocabulary of peace.

We ask God to give us the hope that out of all the pain and grief and agony of so many disjointed and broken lives, a new rebuilding of life and of dreams can take place.

We ask God to give us the strength so that as a people we may begin again to build a bridge of hope into the future. We ask God to deepen our faith so that as the darkness of Calvary awaited the dawn of Easter morning, the darkness of these Omagh days may lead to a new dawn of peace.

May God be with all those still caught in the slipstream of that Omagh bomb, that they may experience the presence of God in their lives, that the healing may continue, and that the longed for peace will become a reality for all our people and for all our religious and political traditions.

NEW YEAR'S DAY
Another chapter

I N today's gospel, there is a great contrast between - on the one hand - the excitement of the shepherds and on the other hand the figure of Mary quietly turning over in her mind the extraordinary experience she had gone through and what it would mean for her. In a sense that contrast reflects our own experience, at this time of the year.

On the one hand the excitement of Christmas and on the other hand the kind of reflection and thoughtfulness that takes over at this time of year. Another year has gone, another year has come, a certain stock-taking is in order.

At the turn of another year we often find ourselves mulling over questions like: How happy am I? How satisfied am I with my work or absence of work?

How do I get on with other people? How well do I live? How long have I got left on this earth? With the turn of another year, a certain sombre thoughtfulness is to be expected.

There is a sense too that there are areas of life that we need to take in hand, areas that this time next year we would like to imagine we will somehow have straightened out or accounted for. And it's because of this sense that we are somehow turning over a new page, opening up another chapter of life, that the subject of new year's resolutions comes up.

Of course the very idea of a new year's resolution is enough to make most of throw up our hands in horror. Because we have made and broken so many new year's resolution in the past, we often have the feeling that the best resolution of all to make at this time of the year is not to make any resolution at all.

But that's ultimately a form of despair, a rejection of the very humanity that Jesus Christ took on himself and redeemed. Because a necessary part of the experience of living a human life is to accept the need to struggle and it's those who accept the struggle who ultimately achieve the satisfaction and joy that life can and does bring.

For instance, whatever happiness or contentment you experienced this Christmas didn't magically fall off the Christmas tree.

It was harvested out of the struggles of the year and the years gone by, out of the commitment and the relationships that you struggled to sustain and to deepen over the course of the year and the years. And without the pain that true struggle brings there will be no harvest.

So it's important for us to make new beginnings; it's important for us to know that failure is part of the human condition; it's important for us to be able to accept and live with our failures; and it's important for us to accept the pain of beginning once again.

So we need all of us to be able to do two things: to accept our failures and, despite our failures, to begin again. I know the areas of my life that are awash with failure. I know what I need to make resolutions about. And no doubt you know the same.

So as we begin another new year, we take the opportunity that this new beginning affords all of us, as the limited and imperfect human beings that we are, to make another effort to reach whatever stage of perfection or imperfection that, with God's help, it is in us to reach.

May I wish you all a very happy new year. And if, for one moment, I could be God, if it was in my power to grant you all just one wish for the coming year, out of whatever wisdom I have gained from my own experience of life the most important wish of all is that all of us, old and young, married and single, husbands and wives, parents and children, that the hurts that in the past have been visited on us by other people and especially by those close to us, that we might learn to accept the reality of that hurt and begin to learn to cope with it.

My prayer for this year is that at least some of us may put behind us the hurts that we have unfortunately learned to cherish.

EPIPHANY
Showing forth

ODAY we celebrate the feast of the Epiphany. The word 'Epiphany' means a manifestation or a showing forth. And what we are celebrating today is God showing himself to the world. Today in the Crib our attention is focussed on the Magi or the Three Wise men, these mysterious, probably mythical figures, who came from the East bearing gifts of gold, frankincense and myrrh. They had followed a star; they had come from the mysterious east; they brought with them exotic gifts.

It's an extraordinary story told in a larger than life way and what is at the heart of it is a way of expressing who this child was. It was, if you like, God's way of pointing up three things about this child in the manger. *Incense* indicated that he was God. *Myrrh*, a precious medicinal perfume, indicated that he was human and *gold* suggested that he was a king as fore-told in the Old Testament. God through the Wise Men was showing himself to all people.

That *was* the Epiphany, but what *is* the Epiphany now? God in the Epiphany we celebrate today, showed himself through the Wise Men and the gifts they brought. How is God showing himself to us now? What epiphany can he link into today?

We believe that in our lives, today and everyday, that God is continually showing himself to us. What epiphanies do we experience? What epiphanies have we experienced? That question in another form is: how does God break through into our lives? how has God broken through into my life and into yours? The problem with most of us is that we have immersed ourselves so much in the concerns and pre-occupations of our day that we become insensitive to the epiphanies of God in our lives.

God is trying to show himself to us, he is trying to break through the obsessions of our lives, he's trying to get through whatever shield that we have succeeded in erecting between us and Him. It could be selfishness or thoughtlessness or a lack of reflectiveness in our lives; it could be work or worries about our families or health or career or whatever.

And what happens is not that God has stopped knocking on the door of our hearts but that we allowed the sound of God to become muffled by the concerns of life and for most of us God hasn't a hope of getting through. And it has to be something exceptional, something crucial before we allow him to penetrate the shield of self-interest of self-concern; it has to be something like the death of a parent or the birth of a child or the day of a marriage, to make us stand back, to sensitise us to what God is saying to us through those experiences.

These are times in our lives when God, in a sense, forces an epiphany on us. But there are other times too, other epiphanies of God that are present every day we live, and we don't even pay attention. If we look closely enough we should be able to see God breaking through:

– in the beauty and grandeur of the world we live in;
– in the caring and sharing that we experience in family and with those we love;
– in the chance meeting or event that suddenly can change an attitude or a perspective on the way we live our lives;
– in the humour and fun and good cheer that we find in those around us, in the joy and excitement on the face of a young child;
– in the love that teenagers express through their music and that they seek in their lives;
– in the quietness and solitude of the elderly as they attend to their prayers and not least in the Eucharist we celebrate and so on.

God is truly in the bits and pieces of everyday. God's epiphanies are all around us if we could only link into them every day we live. The Epiphany that the Wise Men attended to in to-day's gospel is a reminder of the other epiphanies that have taken place down the centuries and are taking place in your life and in mine every day we live.

We pray that we may be able to see and profit from the many ways God is trying to break into your life and into mine.

CANDLEMAS DAY
Light, hope and promise

I always feel that there's something lovely about this time of the year, something refreshing and promising and hopeful. Yesterday we celebrated St Bridget's Day, the first day of spring. Today we celebrate Candlemas Day, a feast that has obvious associations with light and hope and promise.

Everywhere you go people are talking about the great stretch there is in the evenings; about the good weather we're having; even about the snowdrops pushing their way through the clay. Our world is breaking out in another spring, another celebration of light and hope and promise.

And at this time of the year, we become even more aware of how the great dividing line between light and darkness impinges on our lives.

As the evenings get longer, people have more of a chance to do their work on the farm, or to go for a walk, or to savour the changing pattern of life as nature comes into her own for another year.

This changing pattern of light and darkness that's so much part of our lives is used very often in the gospels as signs or symbols of another light and another darkness.

Those who believe in Jesus Christ, live in the light. Those who refuse to believe are uncomfortable in the light, they're more at home in the darkness of the world.

So it's no surprise that the symbol of light stands for the continuing presence of Christ with us in our lives.

The day we were baptised someone held a lighted candle for us, a sign of the life of Christ within us. The day we were confirmed we held a lighted candle for ourselves as a sign of our acceptance of that life of Christ within us since baptism.

On Holy Saturday night the Easter candle is lit in a darkened church as a sign of the resurrected life of Christ coming into the world and breaking up the darkness of sin and on that special night we light our own candles from the Easter candle as a sign of the life and light of Christ within us.

And the day we die we will hold a blessed candle in our hands – or someone will help us to hold it – as a sign of Christ's life within us and as a light to light our path through the darkness of death into the clear light of the happiness of God's home.

So the light is important to us. And the blessed candle is important to us and that's why Candlemas Day, the day of the blessing of the candles is important to us.

Because the blessed candle represents the light and life of Christ, it represents the presence of light and goodness in our lives and in our world and we bring that blessed candle with us through life as something that represents what we believe and what we are.

We need the light of Christ to give a meaning, a purpose, a direction to the often confused wanderings of our lives. When we are helpless, in situations outside our control, we need Jesus to be close to us. When life seems to lose all meaning for us and nothing seems worthwhile or to make sense we need Jesus to say to us 'I came that you may have life and live it to the full.' When we feel discouraged at our own failures and broken by our own sinfulness we need Jesus to say to us 'Come to me all you who labour and are overburdened and I will give you rest' When we feel isolated from others, especially those from whom we expect support and comfort we need Jesus to say to us 'I am with you always'

So today we have a great sense of hope, the hope that comes not just with the turning of another year and the freshness and sense of life that Spring brings but a hope that comes from our faith in the goodness of God and our belief that he is present among us, our belief that the light of Christ continues to burn brightly in our world.

SUNDAY BEFORE LENT
On doing something for Lent

W HEN people went to Mass years ago, most of them had to walk miles to the Church, in good weather and bad weather. And when they arrived there was no heat, the Mass was in a language they couldn't understand, and if the Church was anyway large a lot of the time they couldn't hear what the priest was saying in the sermon. There was no soft padding on the kneelers of the seats and if they wanted to receive Communion they had to fast from the night before. Now things are different. Most people come in heated cars to Mass in heated churches. We have amplification, a one hour fast for Communion.

Now I'm not recalling all that just to glorify the past because the past has its own shadows as well. I'm saying it just to point out how used to comfort and convenience we've become. And whereas in the past we took things like fasting and self-denial for granted, in today's world ideas like fasting and self-denial seem to be out of the Middle Ages.

We can understand people fasting (for instance) for the good of their health or to lose weight because they'd like to get into a favourite outfit. But fasting for a spiritual motive - that seems to be a language that we no longer speak, that's part of a world that has virtually disappeared.

Nowadays most people live relatively comfortable lives. In fact we don't know what we'd do if the electricity was off even for a day, if we hadn't X number of channels on the television, if we couldn't go to the pub X number of nights a week and if we hadn't the facilities that modern life offers us.

And we don't know what we'd do because we've forgotten, many of us, we've forgotten about how to put up with things.

Before this we were more used to putting up with things.

There was a language of self-denial and sacrifice that we knew how to speak but in more comfortable times we've forgotten the words.

And that's why the experience of Lent has practically disappeared for most people. That's why for most people Lent is no more than getting the ashes on your forehead on Ash Wednesday and kissing the cross on Good Friday.

We have airbrushed out of our experience the cutting edge of what Lent is supposed to be.

And when all is said and done Lent is really a time when we confront what we believe. And what we believe, what this church represents, what our presence here today is saying, is that God loves us so much that he sent his Son into this world to make up for the sins that you and I have committed or will commit for the rest of our lives. And during Lent we remind ourselves about Jesus dying on a cross for each one of us and during Lent we respond to that truth by voluntarily doing something that reflects that truth, by voluntarily taking on some activity that reminds us in some graphic way that the crucifixion and death of Jesus Christ is at the very heart of our faith and that that death and crucifixion was a painful and awesome experience of God's love for each one of us.

So what I want to do today is to put before you the challenge and the opportunity that Lent is to bring back into the very centre of our lives the fundamental truth of our faith that God loved us so much that his Son died on a cross for us.

I want to put before you some possibilities for marking that truth this Lent and I'm not going to beat around the bush in making these suggestions:

First I want to suggest to you that for Lent – if you're in good health – and if you're not elderly or a young child I'd suggest that you seriously consider the possibility of dropping one meal a week that you'd normally have, say the dinner on Friday or the tea on Wednesday or whatever.

Now I make that suggestion first because it's the kind of suggestion that Lent brings up because Lent forces us to think about sacrifice and self-denial and in a way Lent is a test of our seriousness about living as God wants us to live.

In other words, what I'm suggesting is that we take Lent

seriously, that we do something that makes us feel the cutting edge of Lent. A few years ago it became popular to *do something* for Lent rather than to *give up something* for Lent. The phrase we used was 'Let's be positive rather than negative. Let's do something rather than *not* do something.'

Well, today I'd like to go against that trend.

So let's give up something, this Lent, something definite, something measurable. Let's give up cigarettes or drink, and let's encourage children to give up sweets or biscuits or whatever.

Whatever it is, pick something that has an edge to it because whatever we do should have sacrifice written all over it. Whatever we do should in some small way remind us of what Lent is all about, the suffering and death of Our Lord and Saviour Jesus Christ for each one of us.

There are, of course, other things we can do too. Maybe going to an extra Mass a week. Maybe making a better effort to say a few morning or night prayers. Maybe buying one of the many good booklets that are now available that help us track a course during Lent.

But whatever we do let's do something that keeps the experience of Lent very directly in our sights. So let's do our best, to do something *real* for Lent, and let's help and encourage those around us to see Lent as a very special time, a *real* opportunity of preparing for our celebrating of the passion, death and resurrection of Our Lord and Saviour, Jesus Christ.

The word *Lent* comes from an old English word for *Spring*. And our key to a proper understanding of Lent is that, like Spring, it is a time of hope, of growth, of renewal, an opportunity for changing ourselves a bit more into what God would like us to be, an opportunity for growing towards God.

So make a good start for Lent by coming to Mass on Ash Wednesday for the holy ashes which will mark the beginning of Lent. And for the rest of Lent, make your own mark on it by choosing some area of real self-denial.

Lent, in a sense, forces a choice on us. By doing something, we're making a statement. By not doing anything, we're making a statement too.

ST PATRICK'S DAY
Taking stock

BIRTHDAYS are important occasions. They help us to take stock of ourselves, to have a look at *who* we are and *what* we are and *where* we are. Birthdays give us a sense of the passing of time, and of course they give us too an excuse for celebrating. Feastdays are the same, especially national feastdays. Like birthdays, they give us an excuse for celebrating and they help us to take stock of *what* we are and *where* we are as a people.

And from year to year, as we know, our stock as a nation can change considerably. Remember, a few years ago, after the Good Friday Agreement how hopeful the national mood was because the future looked so very promising. Then a year later as the parties struggled towards accepting the reality of what they had agreed, that hope and promise were diluted into a vague optimism that things would somehow work themselves out as we hoped and prayed for the kind of compromise that will ensure peace for the future.

Remember too a few short years ago when so many of our young people queued at airports trying to get entry into America, trying to get the precious visas that would allow them to emigrate. And now a few short years later people from other countries are queueing up trying to get permission to work in Ireland.

Now you could say that the signs are good for us as a people and the signs are not good. While we have many things to be proud of as a people, while we can point to the enormous progress that has been made in our short history, not least in the economic progress of the last few years, while we can take great pride in the individual achievements of people like Catríona McKiernan and Sonya O'Sullivan and the Corrs and the Cranberries and all those who grace a variety of international stages with such distinction, we know too that without stability and without peace, the future will be fragile indeed.

We are reminded so often of how fragile this peace is, of how much more needs to be done to achieve a real peace. This is a peace that needs to be worked at continuously, a peace we all need to pray for continuously.

And as we celebrate our national feast-day, in the given circumstances of our time, let us pray for all those working for peace, let us pray for the grace and the dignity of respect and compromise. Because without respect and compromise, no bridge can be built between the two traditions. So, on St Patrick's Day we remember all those who are working for peace.

Of course St Patrick's Day too is a religious feast. We celebrate the feast of our national saint, St Patrick, and as we do we remember the thousands and thousands of Irish missionaries around the world who have literally like the seventy-two in the gospel brought the message of Christ to the ends of the earth. We remember too those other missionaries who built up God's Church around the world. Not the priests or brothers or nuns but the emigrants who made lives for themselves in other countries and who were too missionaries in the fullest sense of the word.

They are part of a long and a proud and by any estimate an extraordinary missionary spirit that is a continuing source of pride to the Irish Church and as we celebrate the Feast of Patrick, we remember them. And we remember too the many things we can be proud of as a Church -the contribution we have made as a Church to the education of the young, to the care of the sick, to the development of our country, to the care and the love and the sacrifice, that is part of the hidden story of parish life.

And on St Patrick's Day we can remember all of that with justifiable pride. But our remembering must not be the selective remembering of those who always want to write straight with crooked lines, so our remembering takes in not just the light but the darkness as well, not just the achievements but the failures, not just the bright centre of the stage but the shadows that linger around the edges.

So we remember too, as part of that shadowland, we remember the children who were sexually abused by clergy and religious and we again ask pardon from them, from their families and from our people - for a trust that was betrayed. We remember the children who were subjected to physical and psychological abuse in orphanages and schools and we again ask pardon from them, from their families and from our people, for a trust that was betrayed. As a church we have much to regret, as a church we have to accept the shadows as well as appreciate the light.

But of course that shadowland is not the whole story and it is unfair to pretend that it is. But it is part of the story, a part that has to be acknowledged. And on the Feast of Patrick, as we remember the long and proud history of the Irish Church we remember both the joyful mysteries and the sorrowful mysteries that are part and parcel of the Irish Church.

And whatever it is that as a people we have thank God for, then surely the time to do it is on our national feast day. And whatever it is we have to ask God's forgiveness for, then surely the time to do it is on our national feast day.

So today in gratitude and in hope we celebrate our Irishness and all that it has given and meant within our country and outside our country and we recognise our failures and our mistakes as a society and as a nation, in what we have done and in what we have failed to do.

We pray for our country that we may be faithful to what we know is right and true and good. And that we may each play our own part in making our country with its possibilities and its limitations what it can be.

HOLY THURSDAY
In Communion

THE great spiritual writer Fr Henri Nouwen was once a chaplain on the great Holland-America, Trans-Atlantic line. On one occasion in a dense fog he was on a great liner that was trying to make its way into the busy port of Rotterdam. In the thick fog, the entry of this great liner into a very busy port was all being organised through radio signals, the fog was that dense. At one stage the priest was on the deck as the captain was issuing directions and as the captain moved nervously about he tripped over the priest in the fog and he said 'For God's sake, Father, will you keep out of my way . . .' Then he thought to himself again and he said, 'On second thoughts, Father, why don't you stick around, this might be the only time I really need you.

I think we're all a bit like that captain of that great liner. God and religion are a kind of insurance policy - not that important when everything is going well but essential if things go wrong, in case we need them.

So we go to Mass, we do our best to say our prayers, we look after the religion thing because, like the priest on the liner in the middle of the fog, you never know when you might need the bit of religion. But most of the time, for most of our lives, we keep the religion thing out there, when the storms gather, and a child is ill or a spouse is going for tests or the Leaving Cert is on and money or influence or power can't buy what we want, then we turn to God and religion. But when the weather is fine and the sun is shining and everyone is healthy and happy we tend to take God and the things of God for granted. And the problem is that there is often a great disconnectedness in us between life and religion. Life is over here and religion is over there and never the twain shall meet unless there's a crisis. And life goes on as if somehow religion is irrelevant to ninety-nine per cent of living.

You see that gap in all sorts of ways: an employer is paying disgraceful wages to his young workers, but he's at Mass and Communion every morning; a worker is taking materials home from work and takes every opportunity to take it easy unless he's closely supervised, but he'd never miss Mass on a Sunday; a husband or a wife is doing every Novena under the sun but God himself wouldn't be able to live with him or her. There's a yawning gap in most of our lives between what we say and what we do. There's so often this great disconnectedness at the heart of our lives.

That's why the event we remember this evening is so important, the first Eucharist. Another word for Eucharist is Communion, a word that has all sorts of inclusive connotations; it's about bringing everyone together, making connections, linking us into one another, getting us to accept responsibility for one another.

And the word Communion is another word for bringing us into unity with God and with one another. And everyone is invited to Communion, everyone is invited to God's table, everyone is invited to take part in the ritual blessing and breaking and giving of bread that is at the heart of human communion, everyone is invited as an equal at God's table, and everyone draws strength from eating at God's table.

It's the one place where no one can pull rank; it's the one place where people can't push their way to the top of the queue because they have money or power or influence; it's the one place where we stand together in simple solidarity as human beings.

We don't know who's going to kneel beside us at Mass, we don't know whose hand we're going to shake at the sign of peace, we don't even know sometimes who people are or where they come from or what sins they've committed, or whom they know or don't know. And it doesn't matter because we're all invited to eat at God's table.

Fr John McCullough wrote somewhere about an elderly parish priest who had great difficulty with a mentally-handicapped child receiving Communion. The priest felt that the child didn't really understand what Communion meant, that the child had absolutely no concept of what in theological terms we call 'transubstantiation' – that's the changing of the bread and wine into the body and blood of Christ. And the old priest was so worked up about all this that he asked Fr McCullough to say the Mass at which this child was to make her First Communion.

And everything went well with the Mass and the little girl came up with her mother to receive Communion and she held out her hand, took the Communion from the priest, broke the Communion in two halves and gave one half to her mother. Fr McCullough noticed that the parish priest had gone into the sacristy and when Mass was over he found the priest very upset.

When the old man had recovered himself he told Fr McCullough that all his life he had said Mass and received Communion but when that child had received on that day, that the old formula of 'blessed, broken and given' explaining what Communion is, that the formula suddenly came alive for him when that child took the Bread that was blessed and broke it and gave it to her mother. 'I doubted,' he said, 'whether that child should receive Communion and she has helped me to break open the mystery of God's love that Communion is.'

And that's what we celebrate today. It's that all-inclusive and all-embracing Communion that we celebrate this evening. It's that privilege of receiving the body and blood of Christ that brings us into Communion with God and with one another. And may this feast help us to break open that great mystery of Communion, Communion with God and with one another.

EASTER SUNDAY
Faith in the resurrection

THERE was once a famous circus performer called Charles Blondin and in his day he performed some extraordinary feats. Once he performed a particularly dangerous act. A wire was strung across a two-hundred and fifty feet wide gorge and blindfolded, he pushed a wheelbarrow across it. A great crowd of people had gathered to see this great feat and they were absolutely silent as blindfolded he pushed the wheelbarrow very carefully from one side to the other. And a great cheer went up from the crowd when he arrived safely at the other side.

In the midst of all the excitement, a young man ran up to Blondin and said 'You're the greatest artist that has ever lived.' Blondin looked at him and asked him 'Do you really believe that much in my ability'. 'I do' the young man said, 'I believe totally and completely in your ability.' 'Very well' Blondin said to him and then he turned to the crowd and said: 'For my next act I'm going to cross the wire again and this time blindfolded I will push this young man in my wheelbarrow.' And of course when he looked around the young man had disappeared.

If we're honest there's a bit of that young man in us all. We can all point to occasions and circumstances where we were carried away with something and we made statements and even sometimes maybe made commitments and then in the cold light of day, we begin to realise that when the emotion evaporates, the cold reality of life soon helps us to make a distinction between what we may say and what we actually believe.

Our faith in the resurrection can be a bit like that too. We can proclaim our alleluias on Easter morning. We can have absolutely no problem affirming our belief in life after death. We can even offer words of comfort and encouragement to the bereaved and those in difficulty. But when our own faith is suddenly put to the test we can soon realise the difference between proclaiming Alleluias on Easter morning and accepting the reality that faith-in-the-risen-Christ demands of me in a given situation.

It can be relatively easy to believe in the resurrection and in the light and goodness of God when children are healthy and life is fulfiling and a marriage is happy and work is going well and when the sun shines for us and for those we love. But when the clouds gather and someone we love is dead or a child is seriously ill or a marriage breaks up or a job is lost - then it's quite a different matter to incorporate that experience into our life of faith.

Many of us too can have this attitude, that if we believe in the Risen Christ, if we do our best to live as well as we can, that therefore everything should work out for us, that all our sicknesses will be cured, that all our young people will pass their exams, that we're all bound to live happy and contented lives, that, in a way, God really owes us that much.

But that's to look at faith from a very limited, human point of view. Faith-in-the-resurrection of Jesus Christ isn't a magic potion that we apply to the great ailments of life and suddenly makes them disappear. Faith-in-the-resurrection of Jesus Christ is a condition or a perspective that gives us both the insight and the courage to face life as it is, to confront the pain of illness, to bear the loneliness of bereavement, to face the cutting edge of personal failure. Faith is about saying: I believe in the sun even when it is not shining; I believe in love even when I am alone; I believe in God even when he is silent.

When life goes against us, when everything seems dark, when we are inclined to turn in on ourselves, like the apostles in the Upper Room in Jerusalem. The Risen Christ calls us to face the reality that life is for us, the Risen Christ calls us to fight the small and the great battles of life; the Risen Christ calls us to give a perspective of light and hope to the inevitable pains and limitations of the human condition.

Our faith in the resurrection tells us that we are empowered by the risen Christ – who turned the disaster of Calvary into the victory of Easter morning – that we are empowered through the light of the risen Christ, to brighten the darkness of our world, to bring courage and hope and strength into whatever set of circumstances we happen to find ourselves.

And we know from our own experience of life, that having the faith and living a good life and saying our prayers and doing this or that novena or going on this or that pilgrimage doesn't automatically mean that everything is going to work out well for us. It doesn't mean that God is going to dot every 'I' and cross every 'T' for us at our bidding. It doesn't mean that faith in the risen Christ somehow inoculates us against the pains and the problems of life.

But what faith in the risen Christ gives us is a reassuring presence, a quiet strength, a perspective on life, a secure harbour out of which we can learn to face and to influence the life that God has given us.

Our faith in the Risen Christ won't make life any easier. It won't make the pain disappear. But it will help us to face with confidence and with courage whatever trials and difficulties we meet in this life. May your faith and my faith in the Risen Christ give us the courage and strength to face, as faith-people, the lives that God has given to us to lead.

We may not be expected to sit in a wheelbarrow while its being pushed by a blindfolded man over a great gorge. But there will be occasions when our faith in the Risen Christ will make real and difficult demands on us. It's then and only then that we'll know how much that faith means to us.

Christ has died! Christ is risen! Christ will come again!

CORPUS CHRISTI
Symbols of God's love

W HEN we lose someone very precious to us - a husband or a wife, a father or a mother, a son or daughter, a special friend – when we lose in death someone we've deeply loved, it's one of the most moving yet very difficult experiences we'll ever face.

We try to make some sense of it, we try to put words on it, we try to use our heads to sort it all out in some controllable way. But the head is no good at a time like that, because it's the heart that wants to be heard.

There are things that we want to say, things that we need to say and only the heart can say them. Words fail us because the emotions, the heart is so strong. And to express how we feel one of the things we sometimes do at a graveside is to drop a red rose on the coffin. It can be a powerful expression of a love that can't be explained in mere words.

It has all to do with the power of symbol. The red rose thrown on to the coffin speaks words of appreciation, of gratitude, of respect but ultimately of love. And it speaks those words not to the people looking on but to the person who does it - the person who actually throws the rose into the grave. That rose speaks not just for that day but the days and weeks and years that have gone before, that rose speaks not just of feelings now but of feelings then, that rose sums up the complicated mixture of regret and guilt and loss and love that we go through when we lose someone precious to us.

And the danger of explaining what the rose means, the danger of milking the symbol of meaning is that we take away from it, we make it ordinary and unimportant. Because we can't explain, as we stand over the grave of a loved one, we can't explain what we feel. In a way you could say that today is like that. The symbol today is not a red rose but a wafer of bread and a drop of wine and the bread and wine, like the rose, have meaning not just for this morning but way back into the past. Back to last Sunday, back to a wedding Mass, back to our First Communion Mass and ultimately back to Calvary and the Last Supper.

We take the bread and wine, symbols of a sacrifice on Calvary almost 2000 years ago, symbols of sustenance for Christians back the centuries, symbols of food for your life's journey and for mine. We take the bread and wine as symbols that speak of God's love for us and symbols that speak of our gratitude, appreciation and love for God.

For just as the rose focuses the unfocussed feelings of the heart, the bread and wine focus not just God's continuing love for us but our continuing need for God.

When Jesus took the bread and wine at the Last Supper and changed them into his body and blood as food for life's journey, he gave us in that time and in that place symbols that have continued to speak to us in this time and in this place.

When priests under the threat of death broke bread in sheltered glens surrounded by people who had risked their lives to attend a hidden Eucharist, the bread and the wine spoke of God's love for them and their need for God.

When we made our first Communion, when married couples exchanged their vows, when we attended the funerals of those we loved, when we celebrate anniversaries or pray for those doing exams or when we ask God to help us out of some difficulty, or when we try to make sense out of life, we often turn to a priest who through the power of God confects the Eucharist, a priest who takes a wafer of bread and a drop of wine and reminds us once again of God's love for us and our need for God.

So on this day, on the Feast of Corpus Christi, the feast of the Body and Blood of Christ, we hold in memory and in gratitude the great Christian symbols of bread and wine that continue to speak to us of God's love for us and our need for God.

ASCENSION
Hope in a hopeless world

I remember one time being called out in the early morning to the scene of a drowning accident. It was that in-between time of morning between dark and light. The sea looked threatening and menacing almost as if, I thought at the time, almost as if it was brooding over a victory. I remember exactly the feeling of desolation that came over me, a feeling of hopelessness, almost a feeling of despair at the mountain of pain that this accident was going to visit on this family. A husband, a father, a son, a brother was dead and for all who knew and loved him nothing could ever be the same again.

At different times in our lives we get that desolate feeling, that awful sense that life is turned upside down, that sense that evil has triumphed over good, that nothing will ever be quite the same again.

How could people just carry on with life as if nothing had happened? How could children go to school? How could people go to work? How could anyone sit down and watch their favourite television programme? How could anything be normal again? When disaster strikes, there is this sense of things falling apart, this feeling that the tried and tested centre isn't going to hold, this idea that nothing will ever be the same again. That's very much what the Ascension experience was on the first Ascension Day.

Jesus ascended into heaven. He disappeared into the clouds and the disciples stood there looking into the empty sky and all they could do was go away and wait, wait for the coming of God's Spirit.

It was a waiting in faith, the kind of waiting that sooner or later is part of the experience of every person. And we know the trials of waiting, waiting at the scene of an accident for a doctor or a priest to come, waiting for the Leaving Cert or the Junior Cert to start, waiting for a baby to be born, waiting even for someone to die.

And all of these waitings are echoes of the great waiting that in faith we are all part of, that waiting for unity with God that comes at the end of life. It's not of course that we always want that to arrive as soon as possible, far from it. There is inbuilt in all of us a desire to go on living life to the fullest for as long as we can. But in a more general sense, behind that normal and natural involvement in living life to the full, behind that is the knowledge that every life is passing away and that the resolution we all hope for after life ends is unity with God.

And we cope with that waiting, as the apostles coped with the waiting for God's Spirit, by not allowing the cares and the worries of life blind us to the action of God all around us or to the destiny that one day we hope to share with the Risen Christ.

So what the Ascension helps us to do is to lift our hearts and minds beyond the worries and cares and sorrows of the present moment to the eternal destiny that God has laid out for each one of us. Now that of course is easier said than done. Someone is dead, someone we loved deeply and intensely and unremittingly and thoughts of the Ascension won't remove the deep sorrow, the terrible grief that almost sweeps us away. Someone we love is very ill, someone close to us is in terrible difficulty and we wonder what the future will hold. And we wonder how we can lift ourselves from the sense of desperation and hopelessness that threatens to engulf us. What, we wonder, can we possibly do to lift the burden of this cross?

And yet extraordinarily out of situations of unimaginable grief, out of the unbroken darkness of the day, a tiny light can begin to shine. Out of the dead soil of a winter's grief, a spring shoot of hope and promise forces its way to the surface. Because that is what the Ascension represents: hope in an often hopeless world.

The message is that out of terrible darkness, a small and flickering light can brighten up the skies of grief and pain. The message is too that as we look into the sky as the apostles did on that first Ascension Day, we realise that, like the apostles, there comes a time when we have to go home. There comes a time when all we can do is, go home. There comes a time when we pick up whatever pieces of life we can and begin to move along the road of life's journey. The truth is that while we never forget, the passing of time, the support of our family and friends and the love of God that serves as an encouraging backdrop to our lives, will in time eventually turn what, like the Ascension, seemed to be a disaster into something that we have to make part of what life is for us.

Because the Ascension, even though it seemed to mark an end, was in truth another beginning. The waiting continues, life goes on and the Spirit of God comes to move among us.

So for all in pain, we pray for consolation and healing, the healing that comes from waiting with God and from the faith that helps us to know that God is carrying us, that he is with us on every step of life's journey.

So, as we celebrate Ascension Day, as we relive again that mixture of hopelessness and promise that the apostles experienced at the Mount of Olives, we pray for the strength and the courage to face whatever the future brings.

And we pray especially for all those who, at this time, sense the hopelessness but can't feel the promise. May this Ascension experience lift their hearts and minds to the promise of God's presence that lies behind it.

PENTECOST
Casting out fear

A NYONE watching Gay Byrne's last *Late Late Show* will
have had a sense of how historic the occasion was. It was
important not just because Ireland's most famous broadcaster
was calling it a day. It was important not just because the
longest running television chat-show in the world was coming to
an end after thirty-seven years. It was important because *The
Late Late Show* and Gay Byrne reflected over the last four
decades a changing Ireland.

The slogan was *It happened on the Late Late Show* and it
usually did because Gay Byrne and the *Late Late Show* were, in
a way, the conduit of so much change in Ireland. Change would
have come anyway but we saw it coming on the *Late Late Show*
and the programme that succeeded in challenging the great
institutions of Irish life eventually became an institution itself.

The Late Late Show on television and *The Gay Byrne Show* on
radio became part of what we are, became part of what we are to
such an extent indeed that Gay Byrne ended up as a reassuring
presence. Programmes came and programmes went,
governments came and governments went, but Gay Byrne
always seemed to be there.

I'm not attempting this Pentecost Sunday I'm not attempting
to compare Gay Byrne to the Holy Spirit – though to some people
he was almost the fourth person of the Blessed Trinity. But on
Pentecost Sunday I'm focussing on just one aspect of his public
life, his constant presence in our lives, a presence that offered
reassurance and comfort and constancy.

And the feast of Pentecost which we celebrate today is about
that too. God offering a different kind of reassurance and comfort

and constancy - Jesus who ascended into Heaven, Jesus sending the Spirit into our lives.

On that first Pentecost Day in the form of tongues of fire God's Spirit came down on the apostles, reassuring them, inspiring them, transforming them from fearful and frightened men into courageous preachers of the gospel of Jesus Christ. And what has that event to say to you and me in this time and in this place? What's the 'relevance' of Pentecost to you and to me now?

There are many answers to that question but I want just to focus on one element. In a way the event and the experience of Pentecost is a parable for our time. Because if we were to ask what's the dominant emotion of our age, what's the personal and social experience without which we would have a greater opportunity to live happy and fulfiled and contented lives? We would mention things like the breakdown of family life or marriage breakdown or the abuse of drink or drugs or the other great personal and social issues that confront us at this time. And important and significant as they are to us today, there is behind them that widespread and debilitating emotion that we call fear.

In that room in Jerusalem two-thousand years or so ago, there was a lot of fear. The apostles were frightened and now in this society, in our families, in our own personal lives there's a lot of fear too. People may say that with the increased prosperity of our times that we really never had it so good but whatever about the good news of our present prosperity and good news it is, we are still left coping with the fears and the doubts that are part and parcel of every life.

Because regardless of whether we've money or we haven't money, whether business is successful or not, whether we've have a job or a life or a future, we're all in different ways victims of fear and of fearfulness. Fear is the great plague of our age and everyone suffers from it. Fear affects the development of children; it torments the teenager; it ravages those in middle-age and it haunts the old.

We're afraid of something all of the time and of everything some of the time. We're afraid of letting people down or been let down. We're afraid to love someone because we're afraid they won't love us. We're afraid of losing our jobs or our health or our friends. We're afraid of ourselves and the harm we're capable of doing. We're afraid of others and what they think of us or might say about us. We're afraid for the world and the terrible things that may happen.

Some of us are even afraid of God who might punish us with eternal damnation. Fear is such a widespread experience of life today that words like anxiety, worry, stress, tension are very much part of the medical and social vocabulary of our time.

So while we wouldn't say that Pentecost, that the coming of the Spirit among us, was just about the casting out of fear, we can see it today as a parable for our own time. Just as the Spirit gave new hope and courage to the fearful and frightened apostle, the Spirit can release each of us from the prison-world of hopelessness and fearfulness and even despair that we can sometimes create for ourselves, or that at least we allow to crowd in on us.

What Pentecost calls us to do is to realise what our Confirmation meant, what the coming of the Spirit has done and can do for us. If we could only open ourselves to the movement of God's Spirit in our lives, if we could allow the Spirit to heal us and to lead us away from the crippling experience of fearfulness and distrust, if we could only allow the Spirit to overwhelm our experience of failure and inadequacy with the experience of love and acceptance then the gifts that the Spirit brought to the Apostles on the first Pentecost, the gifts that the Spirit brought to us in our Confirmation, the gifts that the Spirit continually makes available to us would become real in our lives and would help us to deal with the inevitable fears that are always part of the experience of living a human life.

May we on this feast of Pentecost be more aware of the activity of God's Spirit in our lives and may those who are 'full of fear', for whatever reason, experience on this day the healing power of God's Spirit.

TRINITY SUNDAY
Wonder

THERE'S a story told about an investment banker from the United States who was on holidays in Mexico. And one evening he was sitting at the pier. He saw a fisherman docking his small boat. Inside the boat were several large tuna. The banker complimented the Mexican on the quality of the fish and asked how long it took to catch them. 'About an hour or so' replied the Mexican.

The banker asked him why he didn't stay out longer and catch more fish and the fisherman said he had enough to support his family's immediate needs. The banker then asked 'But what do you do with the rest of your time?' The fisherman said 'Well, I sleep late in the morning, I fish a little around noon, I play with my children for a while, I take a siesta in the evening and then later on I ramble into the village and I spend the evening sipping wine and playing the guitar with my friends.'

The investment banker said. 'Look I'll give you some advice. You should spend more time fishing and, with what you make, buy a bigger boat. Then with what you make from the bigger boat you could buy more boats. Eventually you could buy a fleet of fishing boats. Instead of selling your catch to a middleman you could sell directly to a processor, eventually you could even open up your own cannery. You'd have to leave this little village, of course, and go to Mexico City, Los Angeles or possibly New York if the business continued to thrive.'

The fisherman looked at the banker for a long time and then he asked 'But how long would all this take?' The banker replied 'Maybe fifteen to twenty years.' 'But what would I do then?' the fisherman asked. The banker laughed out loud and said 'But don't you see, that's the best part of it. When the time is right, you could float your company on the stock market, you could sell your stock to the public and become a very rich man. You could make millions.'

And the fisherman asked him 'And what would I do then?' The investment banker said 'Well, then you could retire. You could move to a small coastal village, where you could sleep the morning, fish a little, play with your children, take a rest in the evening, stroll to the village in the evenings where you could sip wine and play your guitar with your friends.' And the fisherman said 'But isn't that what I'm doing now?'

Sometimes there is a truth so close to us that we're not able to see it at all. We're not able, as we say, to see the wood from the trees. Sometimes it's only when we leave home that we begin to appreciate what it offered. Sometimes it's only when we're ill that we realise the value of good health. Sometimes it's only when we lose someone that we realise how much we miss them. And the same is true of religion. We can drift into Mass and out of Mass, we can fulfil what are the public requirements of religion but if we don't attend to God, then we will eventually find that we have drifted away from God and the things of God. And if that happens then one day we'll find that behind the public expression of the practice of our religion, there isn't the depth and the substance and the richness of a lively faith in a personal God.

Because that's what's at the heart of our Christian faith. In the words of the gospel *God loved the world so much that he gave us his only Son*. In other words Jesus Christ died on the cross for you and for me, for your sins and for my sins, for your eternal salvation and for my eternal salvation. But we may be in danger of losing our sense of how central that belief is.

In fact many people nowadays may be losing not just their belief in the Christian faith but their belief in a God at all. And I think part of the reason for that is that so many have lost their sense of wonder.

At certain times in life we get glimpses of this sense of wonder. Like when Manchester United won the great Treble in 1999. It was a great sporting occasion. It was historic in many ways. It was like a great liturgy with thousands of red vestments, the great stadium in Barcelona was like an altar and twenty-two great players were the celebrants. It had its banners and its hymns and like a great religion it had its rituals of one kind or another. But because it was so unique, it left people with a sense of extraordinary wonder that the sum of what happened was somehow greater than all the parts added together. There was some extra dimension that made people pause and say: It was good to be here, it was good to have seen this match.

I would go so far as to say that Barcelona was almost a kind of religious experience in the sense that it somehow encouraged people to look beyond the experience for something that opened them up to wonder. It's like a father or a mother taking their new-born baby in their arms for the first time and sensing that somehow the miracle of birth has opened them up to wonder, a wonder that they sense is not just the wonder of a new human life but a hint of the wonder of God.

Or when some people walk beside the sea on a beautiful summer's day or watch a golden sun set in a golden sky, the wonder they sense is not just the beauty of the world but a hint at the beauty of God.

When people are suddenly overwhelmed by a sense of uncompromising love for someone else, when a musician's control over a musical instrument is such that we find tears in our eyes, when someone sings with the voice of an angel, and we find the hair beginning to stand on the back of our necks, and when something like Barcelona happens, I believe we are given an insight into the spark of the divine that's embedded in human life and we are beckoned in the direction of God.

If one prayer could be answered on Trinity Sunday, my prayer would be that everyone of us, from the youngest child in our faith-community to the oldest person alive, that all of us would get a glimpse of a kind of wonder that would open a chink of light for us into the wonder of God. Because all around us, in the world God has given, in the people among whom we live, there is a spark of the divine that alerts us to the majesty and the splendour and the grandeur of God.

So I pray on Trinity Sunday for a sense of wonder - that we may begin to see that behind the great wonders of life and of living there is a wonder that we call God trying to break through into the bits and pieces of our days and lives. A God who is Father, Son and Spirit, seeks to help us to get a glimpse of the wonder at the heart of the Trinity, Father, Son and Spirit.

ST. PETER AND ST. PAUL
Creative tension

MANY people were very upset when it was announced that Ascension Thursday and Corpus Christi were no longer to be holydays of obligation. The main complaint was that these two feasts have been celebrated as Holydays for such a long time that they had become part of the tradition and practice of the faith of the people, and that change, shifting things around, wasn't such a good idea, that really things should be simply left as they are.

What we forget of course is that change has always been part of the church, that new approaches, different attitudes, developing understanding are not just necessary but essential if the gospel message of Jesus Christ is to be brought into the world we live in and to the succeeding generations that live in that changing world.

Change is not just part of life, change is the essence of growth. Adaptation is not a sign of death. It's a sign of wanting to seek out new forms so that old truths will continue to live. So change is not just something we tolerate in religious matters. Change is something we need to manage, to encourage and ultimately to embrace.

And we do manage and welcome change very well most of the time. For example it's not that long since this feast we celebrate today the feast of Saints Peter and Paul was a holyday of obligation. It hasn't been a holyday for years but we took that change as we've taken most change very much in our stride. And the reason we see change as important, the reason that as a Church we welcome change, the reason that we're able to manage change reasonably well is that we're very aware now that in our church there are different voices offering different opinions on a range of different issues.

For example, some people say that women should be ordained to the priesthood. Others say they shouldn't. Some people say that the laity should be given more responsibility for the running of the Church. Others say they shouldn't. Some people say priests should be able to get married, others say they shouldn't. And so on. Different voices suggesting different things, debating the issues that this century throws up, looking at the old message in a new light, reflecting, pondering, proposing new ideas, new thoughts, new approaches.

Now some people think that that's not the way it should be, that it's all written down in the teaching of the Church and in the law of the Church and that's that. That there's no place for debate, that there's no place for change. Again this feast tells us that there is. You see Peter and Paul never really got on with each other. They were very different people. They had very different ideas about how the Church should be organised. Peter was the leader given by Jesus to the Church and his view was that things should remain as Jesus had left them. But Paul's idea was that there were issues that Jesus hadn't confronted and that you couldn't walk away from them but that you had to bring the mind of Jesus to them.

And that tension remains in the Church to this day, the tension between those who are in positions of authority and their job is to hold the line, to conserve things, not to let things slip, to say: 'This is the way things always were and why should things change?' And they're in creative tension with another group in the Church - those who want to extend the boundaries, those who want to push out into different and deeper waters, those who don't ask why should things change but why shouldn't things change.

And Peter and Paul represent these two different approaches that will forever be in creative tension with one another. And the Church in celebrating this feast is saying to us: we need both the Peters and the Pauls, we need those who conserve and those who question, we need the creative tension between the two approaches. And we need particularly to understand that this tension is there and that this tension will always be there. It's part of the nature of the Church.

A good image for the Church is that of a family making a journey in history. There are certain truths in that family that are so sacred that they become unchanging traditions and there are other truths and traditions that are changeable, that can be changed and that should be changed if that family is going to survive and to prosper. And just as any family will experience a necessary tension between what different members of a family see as acceptable or unacceptable, so the Church will experience the same tension, the same debate between what's essential and what's not essential, between what can be changed and what cannot be changed. And the tension between the various voices is not a sign of death or of decline but a sign of life, a sign of energy and a sign of growth.

And today's feast is a reminder to us of the existence of and the need for that creative tension. We believe that the Church is based on firm and unchanging principle, our beliefs are grounded in the words of today's gospel: 'You are Peter and on this rock I will build my Church, and the gates of Hell can never hold out against it. I will give you the keys of the Kingdom of Heaven whatever you bind on earth will be considered bound in heaven and whatever you loose on earth will be considered loosed in heaven.'

We believe that God has given his authority to his Church, to bind and to loose, to preach the message in season and out of season, and that authority is centred on the successor of St Peter, the sign and the symbol of the authority of Jesus Christ on this earth. And they are the Peters of the Church.

And we believe too that in the family of the Church there are theologians and thinkers whose job it is to hold that authority up to the light, and to listen to the signs of the times and to see how the two can be brought together. To see how our understanding can change and develop, to see how new ideas and new approaches can help the old message find new life in a different world. And they are the Pauls of the Church.

So today the Church reminds us in this feast and we remind ourselves that there will always be a creative tension between the Peters and the Pauls, as we bring the message of Jesus Christ to another generation and to another age.

Saints Peter and Paul, pray for us.

SACRED HEART
The picture on the wall

IF you're my generation or close to my generation then probably one of the memories you'll have with you for as long as you live is of the Sacred Heart Picture on the wall of the kitchen at home and the little red light burning under it. And if the picture was there, and if the red light was burning under it and if it was part of your childhood, that picture and that red light have probably imprinted themselves indelibly on your mind.

There are people now living in New York or Australia or South America or wherever, and there are people who have stopped going to Mass or maybe even saying a prayer but they can still see in their mind's eye that Sacred Heart light burning in their own kitchens forty or fifty or sixty years ago. It is indelibly imprinted on their souls.

Because the wonder is that the images and the lights and the sounds and the smells and the people of our childhoods never leave us. They are packed away somewhere at the back of our minds. And you could be in New York or San Francisco or on the mission fields of Africa or even lost on the far side of the world and then out of the blue you hear a tune on the radio or you get a distinctive smell or you see a face in the crowd or you see a red light shimmering in the distance and suddenly for a moment you're home, you're back again in your own kitchen and we're all warming our hands at the kitchen fire.

Psychologists and other experts tell us what we all instinctively know, that the influence of childhood and home is the greatest influence of all and that it remains with us for the rest of our lives. And that's how belief in God or a sense of God and the things of God or a spiritual dimension to life that's how it moves down from generation to generation, not handed on as such but picked up from the atmosphere of home, picked up from the experiences of community, picked up from the direct message and the oblique remark, picked up from the experiences of childhood and home that gell into a series of values and beliefs.

We know that to be true because some of us have, as we say, been there and done that. We've knelt in a kitchen saying the Rosary – not always, not maybe that often – but we've been there. We know what it's like to look through the rails of a kitchen chair as we knelt with father and mother and brothers and sisters.

We can still see the geography of the kitchen, and the red light twinkling on the wall. We know what it was like to be brought to Mass, almost as soon as we were able to walk. We remember being taught the Hail Mary at home, even when we hadn't a clue what the words meant. We remember that first trip to Knock and how the notion of pilgrimage was born inside us. We remember the breathless excitement of First Communion, and the more steadied experience of Confirmation, and these and so many memories are packed inside us, running little tapes in our heads that come on from time to time and remind us of that sense of God and the things of God that is at the very core of our being.

In a way, for some of us, we cannot but believe because it is so much part of us, so indelibly imprinted on our minds and the tapes just keep on running. It's a strange thing, this childhood influence, some things we never forget. We never forget the words of the Hail Mary and even though people are away from Confession for years on end they still remember the Act of Sorrow and everyone has the tape of the Hail Holy Queen ready to roll inside their heads, if someone gave them a run at it.

We never forget because the images and the sights and the sounds of childhood stay with us for as long we live. The question now is: what are the images that will stay with the present generation? What are the tapes that will be running around in their minds in 30 or 40 or 50 years time?

Now it's not unusual for children to make their First Holy Communion without ever being to Mass. Now it's common for children to come to school without even knowing how to bless themselves. Now it's almost taken for granted that there are few if any religious objects in the homes. The Sacred Heart picture and the crucifix are being replaced by some equivalent of the four ducks flying up the sitting-room wall. Now there is a place in the home for the fridge and the mountain bike and the computer and the Play Station – and thank God for the prosperity that allows us to have them – but where is the place for God, where is the sacred place that will sew the knowledge of God's presence or the seed of God's love into the minds of the young.

God forbid that we wouldn't send our children to school or that we wouldn't bring them to a doctor if they were sick. And yet parents who love their children dearly and who have themselves the precious gift of faith, parents who have a sense of God and the things of God and yet instead of making sure that their children can receive and acknowledge this gift – the greatest gift after life itself that they can give their children – so many are letting it slip, like sand, through their fingers.

People who have had an experience of a parent suffering from Alzhiemer's will know that terrible day when a father or mother, much-loved and much loving for so many years, and one day they look blankly at you and they don't know who you are. And I sometimes wonder will there come a time for a future generation of our people, will there come a time when we will have so lost touch with our faith, even with a spiritual sense, that we may not know who God is even though God in his love and care will always know who we are.

So maybe this third millennium of Christian faith, maybe now is the opportunity to remind ourselves of the need for us to make sure that we ourselves and the children growing up in our parish, that we make sure that there is in our lives and in our homes a sacred space that reminds us of God and the things of God.

We should never underestimate the importance of the visual in the home or the impact the visual makes on the young. So we should ensure that in every home, there is some religious object, some sacred space that will witness to our sense of the presence of God among us. Something that will help us to place a focus on what is at the heart of life, our belief that God loved us so much that he sent his Son to die for our sins.

Is there a greater gift that any parent can give to a child?

THE ASSUMPTION
Making it possible

ROGER Ballister holds a special place in athletics history. He was the first man to run a mile in under four minutes. At the time, it was an event of great significance because at the time, it was an extraordinary achievement. That particular run is important now not because it's regarded as a great achievement anymore but because it set a headline for other athletes. His achievement spurred other runners to greater things.

Eamonn Couglan, John Treacy and Sonia O'Sullivan also have broken psychological barriers for other Irish athletes. What seemed impossible is now, after all, possible. And not just possible but almost expected as the pressure of public expectation puts additional stress on athletes.

But what have Roger Bannister and Sonia O'Sullivan to do with the Feast of the Assumption? Well, you could say that what Roger Bannister did for middle-distance runners and what Sonia O'Sullivan did for Irish women athletes, Mary, the Mother of Jesus, did for those who struggle to live good lives, those who sometimes, in the most desperate of situations, struggle to make sense out of the confusion and compulsions of life.

What Mary is important for and what we celebrate today is that she made possible the kind of life and the kind of living that for many of us much of the time seems to be humanly impossible. What she has done is to make it possible for us to believe that the Christian way of life can be lived to the fullest. Another way of putting it is to say that she has placed the possibility of living a full Christian life on the human agenda.

So we call Mary 'a model of faith'. What we mean is that it's possible, even in the most desperate of circumstances, to believe and to continue to believe and that through that belief we can come close to God and we can live good lives. We sometimes feel 'Well, it was different for her'. After all, she literally had breakfast, dinner and tea in the presence of Jesus Christ.

But we must be careful not to re-read back into history what Mary later came to know about her Son. What we're sometimes inclined to forget is that Mary, at that time, had little idea of what the whole thing was about. She had responded to God's call with faith and trust but with little knowledge. And her faith was really all she had to go on.

As a young woman she gave birth to a child who wasn't her husband's and we can only imagine the problems that that experience involved. As the child Jesus grew up she could not ever really have understood that her Son was, as we know him now to be, the Second Person of the Trinity. When he grew up he left her and went about the country preaching and teaching a strange message and getting into trouble with the authorities. And finally she watched from a distance as he carried the cross on which he would be crucified to a place called Calvary.

And as she watched her Son die she must have wondered why God expected her to endure such agony, why God had allowed her son to die nailed to the Cross like a common criminal. But despite the mystery of it all she accepted even what she didn't understand. And she lived out her life with a firm faith in the love and goodness of God and she was rewarded in her assumption into Heaven with eternal union with God.

In the difficulties of life, when death or sickness comes to family or friend,when things go against us in work or in our personal lives,when we are troubled and distressed by our own failures and inadequacies, Mary, the Mother of Jesus, is the model for each one of us. She's an example of someone who believed and trusted in the love and goodness of God.

Like Roger Bannister or Sonia O'Sullivan, Mary, if you like, is the one who has given us the headline to follow. She's the one who, in the most difficult of circumstances, believed and trusted in the love and the goodness of God. Mary is the headline that helps to encourage us and reassure us through the trials and the upsets of life.

ALL SAINTS
Ordinary people

I want to tell you about someone I knew once. I was a priest at the time but not long a priest. And at a Sunday Mass I was preaching a sermon about baptism. I mentioned in passing that at one time the Church had believed in Limbo, that Limbo was a place of separation from God, that Limbo was a place for babies who died without baptism. There was Heaven and there was Hell and there was Purgatory. And adults went to one place or other when they died and then there was this place called Limbo for unbaptised babies.

And I went on to say that this place in fact never existed. I went on to say that there was no basis in Scripture for believing in Limbo and that the Church no longer believed that unbaptised children who died were separated in any way from God. Innocent babies who died, I said, being without sin, were now in the presence of God for all eternity and that as they were saints with God people should pray *not* for them but *to* them.

There was nothing remarkable in what I had said. It was no more than a statement of a very obvious truth. An innocent child, who died without committing a sin in his or her life, that child has to be in the presence of God, that child has to be in Heaven.

After Mass an old woman came into the sacristy. An old woman, I remember, dressed completely in black. Let's call her Mary and Mary told me that she had six children, four were stillborn, a fifth was a little girl who had lived for about a year or so and a son with whom she now lived. And Mary told me that her four still born children were buried in the field beyond the haggard because the priest wouldn't allow them to be buried in consecrated ground, in the graveyard.

And every morning of her life, the first thing Mary did when she got up was to go to the window and look out over the field beyond the haggard, and pray for her unbaptised children whom she had been told would never see the face of God. And every morning, she had looked out over the graves of her children and prayed that one day they might indeed see the face of God.

And she told me that my words had lifted a great burden off her mind and that from now on she could pray to her children, not pray for them because now they were with God and that meant everything to her. Everything.

This small almost insignificant little woman who had carried this great burden of pain for so long and at such cost, with tears welling in her eyes, told me that I would never ever understand how much what I had said had meant to her. And then she composed herself, wiped her tears away and walked out of the sacristy.

A few months later she was dead. And naturally enough at her funeral I said nothing to anyone about what she had said to me that day in the sacristy. But her son told me later that when they went through her things after the funeral, they found hidden away in the top shelf of her wardrobe a pair of little shoes, her little daughter's shoes, the little girl who had lived for a year. Her son was very upset about it. He was upset that more than forty almost fifty years after the death of that little girl, she had kept the little pair of slippers, and what upset him was that he never knew that she still lived with that sense of loss.

I remember at the time wondering whether I should tell him about the stillborn children, his brothers and sisters who were buried in the field beyond the haggard, because clearly he knew nothing about them. And I decided not to, why I'm not sure.

Part of it was that Mary had taken me into her confidence and I had no permission from her to break that confidence. Part of it too was that I didn't want him to carry a burden that had already been carried for far too long. And part of it, to be honest, was that I was ashamed that my church, of which I was a public representative, that my church had demanded so high a price of this small, delicate but dignified old woman.

And I mention Mary and her still born children today because I want to remember them on the Feast of All Saints. Because that's *what* they are – saints of God. And that's *where* they are, in Heaven, enjoying the fullness of God's presence.

And I wonder too how many more Marys there are. How many more Marys went to the equivalent of that window, every morning of most of their lives and looked out over the equivalent of the field beyond the haggard? How many more Marys took down the equivalent of the little girl's slippers from some wardrobe and ran their fingers gently over them to evoke a memory or just to keep a presence alive? How many more people have carried silent burdens for years on end, burdens of loss or regret, burdens of disappointment and failure, burdens of grief and almost sometimes too, burdens of despair.

And yet they kept going, doing their work, rearing their families, saying their prayers, living out their lives in whatever set of limited circumstances they happened to find themselves. And we don't normally call them saints because we were so familiar with them. We knew them ourselves, we worked with them, they lived down the road, they were part maybe of our own families.

We don't see them as saints like St Anthony or St Francis or St Someone. They were our Mary or your John or Tom who lived down the road. They were ordinary people, mothers and fathers and uncles and cousins and neighbours and friends but they had about them that sense of God and the things of God that turned ordinary lives into graced experiences of the presence of God. They were, as we say, touched by God. So let's pause just for a moment and think of the saints we know, those who are now happy with God, and who wait to welcome us into the heavenly Jerusalem that God has prepared for all of us.

DEATH IN NOVEMBER
Accepting reality

DURING the week we buried the late Michael Crosby of Lisnarawer. Someone said to me after the funeral how impressed they were with the attitude of the people of this area to funerals, to the way we deal with death, to the respect there is for the event that dying is, for the support that people give the grieving. And it is true. Even though we take it for granted, even though it comes second nature to us, we have a feel for the rituals of death and dying that is the envy of many another.

I remember someone who worked in Scandinavia telling me once that a colleague at work seemed a bit upset one day after lunch. When he enquired what was wrong, he was told that the young man had buried his mother that morning. A few hours later he was back at work. It would be unthinkable in our culture.

In Ireland, particularly in rural Ireland, when someone dies, the event is deeply respected. People stop working. Near neighbours instinctively gather to free the family for their grieving, to tend the social necessities, to dig the grave. There is in Ireland too more of a sense of the reality of death. We have the wake and the removal and the Mass and then the graveyard. People cry and we accept that people cry and all of that is so important because all of that helps us face the reality of what death is.

In other countries death is sometimes camouflaged more and, as a result, death becomes more difficult to deal with. An American was once visiting Ireland and he was fascinated to witness a funeral in Donegal. In the graveyard the neighbours filled in the clay over the coffin and at the end they tapped the clay down with the backs of the shovels. And this man said the point that was being made was that this person was dead, really dead and the ritual of filling in the clay was difficult to witness for those grieving but in the long run would help them to accept that death as a reality.

More recently in Ireland we have started to follow trends in other places and the experts would say that it won't serve us well. That part of the reason why we deal with death so well in Ireland is that we don't try to camouflage the fact that a death has actually taken place. And part of the difficulty of dealing with death is that we don't want to face it. We don't even want to think about death and about dying. We prefer to see it as far away and distant, something that has to do with extreme old age, when limbs are tired and constitutions weak, when death is almost natural, like a ripe apple falling off a tree.

But death doesn't wait for old age. We know that. The hard fact of life is that we don't know the *when* or the *how* or the *where* of my death or yours. But one thing we do know is that it will happen. Someday we will be carried into a church in a coffin; someday someone will stand at our graves. Not indeed that we should go around always talking about dying or moping about it or waiting for death to come. But at the same time we know that the person who tries to push aside the reality of death is someone who'll make a poor job of life.

Why is it that today – more than ever before – more and more people want to forget about death and about dying? Part of the problem is that we seem to have less faith in the hereafter, less certainty about the next life. And if we're unsure of what's going to happen when we die, then we'll tend to be fearful of the prospect of dying and of the reality of death.

Because there is somehow built into the makeup of every human being, the need, the wish, the desire to believe that death isn't the end, that there has to be something more that would answer the questions that life asks of us. And it's when we lose that sense of resurrection then we simply turn away from death, we try to push it out of our minds, because it doesn't make sense.

And we can only make sense of death, we can only come to terms with it if we believe that somehow, somewhere there is a reason, a purpose, a meaning behind the contradictions and strangeness of life and of death.

But even if we believe in the resurrection from the dead, even if we believe very clearly and very firmly that we will be happy with God in heaven when we die, that doesn't mean that we can take death easily in our stride. Because there is about death a finality and a completeness that can be very frightening. And there is too of course the human sadness of parting with those we love and a strangeness about death that tends to make us want to shut it out.

We can't image death. We can't imagine what it might be like. And there is too the fact that our faith tells us very little about what happens when we die – apart from unity with God or separation from God. So for all those reasons, most of us most of the time prefer not to think about death or about dying.

Someone asked me when I came here would I be here until I died or retired. I was a bit taken aback at the time because I felt I was reasonably young so I didn't want to start picking my spot beside all the Canons outside the door there on the left.

But we do get uncomfortable with the whole subject of death and it is natural not to want to talk about it. And yet it's so much part of life, it's so much part of the reality of what we are, that maybe during the month of November we might try to stand back a bit from the lives we're living and situate them in the context of death. Not in any morose way. Not getting depressed about it but just in some sense naming it for ourselves, putting it in the context of what we believe about the resurrection of Jesus Christ, putting it too maybe in the context of what we find difficult to believe about the resurrection of Jesus Christ, putting it too in the context of those who have gone before us, those who have walked through the door of death.

IMMACULATE CONCEPTION
God's gift to us

ONE of the points of difference between Catholics and
Protestants is in the matter of devotion to Our Lady. That's
not to say that Protestants have no devotion to Our Lady. Some
of them have, particularly those who are what we'd call High
Church Protestants. Sometimes we think that Protestants are all
the same. Far from it. Anglicanism is a broad church. You have
quite a variety of attitudes and beliefs from those who are,
roughly speaking, what we call High Church – that's those who
are close to the Catholic Church – and those who are Low
Church – those not so close to the Catholic Church.

And there are two opinions that tend to create this impression
of division. One is when Catholics believe that Protestants have
no respect for Our Lady and the other is when Protestants
believe that Catholics think Our Lady is almost God. There is of
course no truth in the Catholic rumour that Protestants have no
respect for Our Lady. And there is of course no truth in the
rumour that Catholics regard Our Lady as God, as almost one of
the persons of the Trinity.

But, at the same time, you can see how that rumours might
start. In Ireland Catholics have traditionally had a very strong
devotion to the Blessed Virgin. There are a number of reasons for
this. One is that in times of persecution, during the Penal Laws
for example, when Mass was difficult indeed dangerous to get to,
people substituted the Rosary as the great community and family
prayer.

And indeed it was the Rosary that helped keep the faith alive
in many parts of Ireland in difficult times. Another reason why
there is such devotion to Mary is that while we have always

believed that Jesus was fully human, there is a kind of feeling around that suggests to us that because Jesus is God, therefore his humanity is somehow different from ours.

And as a result many people have felt more at home in praying *through* Mary than in praying directly *to* her Son. And indeed as a result of that approach, sometimes you will find people paying more attention to Mary than they do to her Son and actually praying more to Mary than they do to her Son.

Now that's getting things the wrong way round. Mary is honoured in our Church because of the part she played in the birth and life of her Son and our Saviour. What I'm saying is that we have always to approach Mary in the context of Jesus and not Jesus in the context of Mary.

It has been said that what we *are* is God's gift to us and what we *become* is our gift to God. What is special about Mary is not just that she was conceived free from all sin but that she accepted God's gift to her in what she *was* and she responded by giving her life to God in what she *became*. It's not helpful to turn Mary into some kind of a goddess as if what she *was* and what she *became* were somehow automatic.

Mary was a young ordinary girl living in a society that didn't take kindly to any suggestion of sexual indisgressions of any kind and she was asked by God to become the Mother of the Messiah. It was a strange and frightening proposal for a young girl. It demanded a life lived literally in the presence of God. It had its share of bewilderment and understanding, conflict and comfort, joy and sorrow. And we honour Mary because of what God asked her to be and because of what she as a person became.

And to turn Mary into more than that or different from that, to imagine that we pray to her in herself rather than through her to her Son, is to turn Mary into something she is not and something which the Church tells us she is not.

So when we celebrate a feast like the Immaculate Conception, what we are celebrating first of all is the important part Mary played in all of our lives. And in the feast of her Immaculate Conception, we are reminded that God has given each one of us an eternal destiny -that is God's gift to us - and we, like Mary, can become our gift to him by living out in our lives the values and the qualities that marked the life that Mary lived.

VOCATION
Shepherding

T HIS day every year we celebrate what we call "Good
Shepherd" Sunday or Vocations Sunday. And in today's
Church and in today's Ireland, we come to Vocations Sunday
with very mixed emotions. In the past few years we've had to
deal with the problem of child sexual abuse by priests and
religious. We've had accusations of physical and psychological
abuse directed at nuns. Add to that the effort that were made to
cover up things, the failure to deal with these problems over the
years. Add to that again the decline in the Church's authority as
a result. Add to that again the surveys indicating the decline of
the practice of the faith. And add to that again the bad
treatment the church often, though not always, receives from
the media.

Put all of that together and what you get is a picture of a
Church in crisis. Put all of that together on Vocations Sunday
and the question we're left with is: in present circumstances why
would anyone want to become a priest or a nun now?

When I went to Maynooth, more than thirty years ago, it was
a very different world. It was unthinkable that anyone would
miss Mass on a Sunday and if they did, the missionaries came
every few years to round them up. It was unthinkable that the
local priest not to mind the authority of the Church would be
questioned in any way. It was unthinkable that someone wanting
to become a priest or a nun would receive anything but support
and respect from family, from neighbours and from friends. And
signs on it.

When I went to Maynooth in 1966, the place was full. Now
the place is emptying by the year and that has changed because

change is all around us. And part of that change is that the Church has lost a lot of its power, and that in some respects may be no harm at all. Part of that change is that the numbers of priests and religious are dwindling, with fewer going forward and more leaving. Part of that change is that attitudes to religion and to the Church have significantly changed.

The Maynooth I went to was full of confidence, full of certainty and full of seminarians studying for the priesthood. Nobody questioned whether compulsory celibacy was a good thing. Nobody even considered that women might be ordained. Nobody asked what seem very obvious questions now. The Maynooth I went to was a staid and settled and secure place. It was a world where every question had an answer, where ever problem had a solution, where we had security and certainty for the breakfast every morning and now more than thirty years later the wheels seem to be coming off.

And in that kind of context, we celebrate Good Shepherd Sunday. We remind ourselves about the need for vocations to the priesthood and to the religious life and some of us wonder will anyone go forward anymore and, if they don't, we sometimes feel who could possibly blame them?

And yet I didn't go to Maynooth, I wasn't ordained, I didn't stay in the priesthood because it was just something I *wanted* to do. I went to Maynooth, I was ordained and I stayed because in a real sense I felt it was something I *had* to do. And that's what we mean by 'call' or 'vocation.' Something stirred in me about priesthood. Why it did I can't fully explain. Why me is an even greater imponderable. And there were times in Maynooth and there were times since ordination when I felt like walking away from it, when I felt that I could be a happier even a better person without the burden of unreason and inconvenience that a vocation brings with it.

So priesthood is about call. It's about hearing, whether we want to hear it or not, God asking us to follow him in the priesthood or the religious life. And it's not about perfection and it's not about being better than anyone else and it's not about wanting to be on a pedestal and it's not about looking for position or respect or adulation, and God help us if we think it is.

Priesthood ultimately is about a particular life of service in answer to God's call. It's about recognising that someone has to pour water over babies to welcome them into God's family; someone has to break the bread of life at God's altar as food for our journey; someone has to represent the compassion of Christ in the confessional; someone has to be there to help us leave this life with the dignity and respect due to us as children of God; someone has to lead God's people in worship; someone has to serve God's family in season and out of season.

And priesthood and the religious life are ultimately about call, about vocation, about wanting to do it because it won't feel right if you don't, wanting to do it because you'll never be really happy if you don't.

And the problem now is not that God's call is not there anymore. The problem is that it's almost impossible now for that call to be heard. There was a time when everyone listened for that call, there was a time when everyone supported those who thought they heard it, there was a time when the climate was fair and the we had the wind on our backs and our parents and families and friends were delighted. But that time has gone.

Now young people don't want to listen in case they hear God calling them. Now if they say that they want to be a priest or a nun, their parents are anxious, their brothers and sisters are embarrassed and their friends think we're for the birds. Now they have the wind on their faces and the hill rising against them and people telling them that religion 'isn't cool' any more and that becoming a priest or a nun doesn't make sense anymore.

But the truth is that it never made sense. Priesthood and religious life, of their very nature, make no sense at all in human terms.

But yet the call is there. And whatever about the world we live, whatever about the limitations and the failures of priests and nuns, whatever about the problems of the Church, we owe it to those who hear the call to make it possible for them to follow it. That's what Good Shepherd Sunday or Vocations Sunday is all about. Helping people to understand that God is calling them, and to give them the support and the encouragement they need to answer that call.

So our prayer today is that God's call may be heard in this community and that that call may not go unanswered.

MISSION
Sharing the gift

TWO weeks ago in Western Australia the death took place of Sr Fergus Kennedy. She was 89 years of age. Josie Kennedy was born in 1910 in the townland of Glan and she was baptised in Kilglass Church. When she was just 17 years of age, she left Glan, in 1927 and travelled to Western Australia to join the St John of God Sisters. She had already two half-sisters in the nuns in Australia and she was later joined by two more sisters, Kitty and Jenny.

The question of course is: why early in this century five sisters from one family in the townland of Glan would go to the other end of the world and spend their lives in the service of God and his church?

What explains it is the word 'Mission' and what explains the word 'Mission' is a sense of how *precious* and *important* is faith in a loving and a caring God. What makes people give their lives at the far end of the world, what makes people live in different cultures and often in difficult circumstances, is their belief in how precious and how fundamental is a sense of God and the things of God. People go on the Missions because they want to share this exquisitely precious gift. People go on the Missions because they want to share the gift of the Good News of Jesus Christ. And that Good news is that God loved us so much that he sent his Son into the world to make up for the sins we have all committed and that because God loved and loves us so much, that he will take us to the happiness of his home when our days in this world are over.

And what this understanding of life gives us is a sense of how important and precious a gift it is to know and to believe that, above and beyond the concerns of this life, there is another life with God that gives meaning and substance to the often confused and complex and unpredictable lives that we lead.

You can call that precious gift a lot of different things. You can call it 'faith' or you can call it or 'a sense of God and the things of God' or you can call it 'a sense of a spiritual dimension to life.' But whatever words we put on that gift, it is *precious* and it is *fundamental* and above all, it is *real*. So real that people, for centuries, people like the Kennedy sisters in Glan, missionaries have left family and friends and place and travelled to the other ends of the world to share that precious gift with others.

And today on Mission Sunday we recognise the contribution that the thousands of Irish missionaries all over the world today have made and are making to the work of Mission, to the work of sharing that precious gift of God's love all over the world today.

Go literally anywhere in the world and up the road a few miles is an Irish priest or a nun or a lay person working away often in what seem like depressing circumstances, often against apparently insurmountable odds and there they are from North Mayo or West Sligo, building churches, opening schools, organising health care, miles from home in a culture and in a climate very different from what they were used to.

So on Mission Sunday we remember them, we pray for them, and we contribute to the work they do. But there's another side to 'Mission' too. This precious gift that missionaries go to the other end of the world to give to people they never met, this gift is something that now we need to bring to each other. I was talking recently to a young couple with a young family who don't practice their religion. Or at least who don't practice their religion, in the sense of going to Mass and they said to me 'We don't go to Mass but don't get us wrong we have the faith.' And they have, no doubt about it. But my question for them was: 'If your children never go to Mass will your children have the faith?'

They would be appaled if someone suggested that they wouldn't send their children to school, or that they might neglect their children's health. But here is the precious gift they have of a sense of God and the things of God, a precious and a beautiful gift, that they could give their children and they are letting it slip like sand through their fingers.

Parents are the first missionaries. If the missioning doesn't happen at home it won't happen anywhere else. Because in a real sense each one of us opens up the precious gift of God's life and God's love to one another.

Mission is you and me in the way we relate to other people, in the attitudes and the values that we live by, in the influence we bring to bear on each other.

Mission is a parent explaining to a young child that some things are right and other things are wrong.

Mission is a teenager prepared to stand his or her ground rather than simply fall in with a prevailing culture.

Mission is someone who at some cost is prepared to stand up for those maybe not able to stand up for themselves.

Mission is people, like you and me, ordinary people living ordinary lives, who are prepared to stand against the prevailing currents of life and give witness to what we believe.

Mission is standing for specifically Christian values at a time and in a world where those values are often seen as old fashioned and out-of-date.

And in a way the greatest missionaries of all are the missionaries who never leave home. I remember some years ago visiting a home and the parents of a young man in his late teens were giving out to him for not going to Mass. Then later the father was talking about cars and he mentioned in passing that he had stopped the speedometer so that the car wouldn't register the number of miles it had travelled. The reason, he said, was that when he came to trade it, he'd get a better price for it. There was a silence for a moment until eventually his son said very loudly 'And he's the man worried about me not going to Mass.'

Home is where Mission starts. A child making his or her first Communion can bring a family back to church; a teenager with a raging sense of justice and fair play can help give a wider dimension to the faith of parents; a business-person by just doing the right thing can steady another young business-person who might be inclined to cut a few corners; a neighbouring couple by going to Mass every weekend can act as a spur to a couple down the road who have got out of the habit; and teenagers, for good or for ill, bring the greatest influence of all to bear on other teenagers. So we are all missionaries. We are all breakers of bread of God's life for those around us.

COMMUNICATIONS
What we say, what we do

W E often hear it said that nowadays the world is a terrible place. And what we mean is that in comparison to the world most of us grew up in, the world now *seems to be* a terrible place. There seems to be nothing but war and violence and killing and disrespect and sexual permissiveness and, if we want to put religious terms on it, what we call it *sin*.

The implication is that the world we knew once was a better and happier and a more pleasant and a more moral place to live in. But on balance that's probably *not* true. The difference is not between a happy and a wholesome world of the past and an unhappy and unwholesome world now. The difference is in what we knew *then* and what we know *now*.

The late TD Oliver J Flanagan once memorably said that before *the Late Late Show* came along there was no such thing as sex in Ireland. What he was saying in effect was that the coming of television had changed our perspective on the world. And it had. What it did and what it does is provide us with information. It allows us to see for ourselves. So years ago when de Valera or John A. Costello spoke in the Dáil, if you were Fianna Fáil you read about it in *The Irish Press* and if you were Fine Gael you read about it in *The Irish Independent*. Now when Bertie Ahern or Michael Noonan talks in the Dáil we see it on television in our own homes and we can see how convincing they are. We can see the white of their eyes; we can note the hesitation or the waffling or whatever; we can see for ourselves.

But television doesn't just give us information. It also tries to change our minds. It almost invariably has something to sell. In modern language television puts a spin on things. And that's the value and the limitation of television and the other communications media available to us today. They give us information but they try to shape our opinions by pushing that information through a particular sieve, by giving that information a particular slant.

And that's why every year, we set aside a particular weekend to focus our thoughts on the communications media and we remind ourselves of the extraordinary power and influence of modern media. We remind ourselves that television is probably the single most powerful influence in our society. It's the platform on which elections are won or lost; it's the medium through which we get most of our information; it's the great former of opinions, the great changer of attitudes, the great influence on decisions. And for that reason it's very important that we're aware of the power and influence of television and the media; it's important that we understand how television operates; how points of view are got across; how communication is taking place even though we don't realise it.

We know that news can be slanted, that statistics can be presented in illogical ways, that the truth isn't always served, that honesty and integrity are as difficult to achieve within the media as in other walks of life. And because television and other media are so powerful and so influential and so persuasive we need to be aware of that and to understand that and to know how it works.

So our prayers today are especially with those who are involved in the communications media that their influence may be for the good and the true and the right. We pray too for all those involved in the wider fields of communication, who try to communicate Christian values and attitudes. For instance we should pray for priests whose job it is to break God's word for God's people - not an easy thing to do. (Some people say we should pray for those who have to listen to sermons, but that's a different point altogether.) And we should certainly pray for parents. Because in the long run this is where real communication takes place. Because if parents don't communicate the person and the message of Christ to their children nobody else will be able to do it.

Because the difficult truth is that in every home some kind of communication is going on. For example, there is no such thing as a neutral home when it comes to religion. Either God and the things of God are special or not special. So what matters to your family is not so much what I say during this Mass but what's being said in your home, what's being said even if no one is saying anything! And not so much what's being said as what's being done because actions, as we know, speak louder than words.

In the long run, it's what we do, not what we say, that influences other people, that communicates a message. The children who know how to pray are those who have learned it in their own homes; the children who go to Communion are those who see their parents going to Communion. Of course it doesn't always work out that smoothly or automatically but there is sufficient truth there to merit our attention.

So we should remember the importance of parents as communicators of values and attitudes and standards for their children.

So we remember parents today as probably the most important communicators of all, of the person and the message of Jesus Christ. And we remember too all those in positions of leadership because of the great trust that has been given to them and the great influence they can bring to bear on other people.

For instance, teenagers bring such influence to bear on each other and the same can be said for everyone whose actions and standards are influencing for good or for ill those around them. That's the most important message that anyone will communicate, a message that we should see not as a burden but as a privilege.

So we pray, on Communications Sunday, that God may direct and bless all those responsible for communication in our world and particularly that God may be with us in our efforts to communicate him in our world, in our place and in our time.

TEMPERANCE
Keeping a balance

TODAY we celebrate Temperance Sunday. It's the day of the year when we look at a virtue that has had a bad press in recent times. The word *Temperance* has all kinds of negative associations now. When we hear the word *Temperance* being used we think of words like spoilsport, not having a good time, something boring and depressing, something at odds with words like excitement, happiness, passion, living life to the full.

And the reason why the word *Temperance* has so many negative associations now is that the world we live in is out of tune with what temperance represents. Temperance is about moderation and control. It's about having a balance in your life; it's about being able to stand back and see where our lives are unbalanced, where our lives are out of control in some sense. And that's difficult to do today because the ethos of our time is about saying *Run with the flow, Don't be negative, Go for it*, and so on. And the flow of life today is in the direction of having a great time and indulging ourselves and getting loads of money and owning property and having a great time and having everything we want and spoiling ourselves. And words like *moderation* and *control* and *balance* these words don't fit easily into the world we live in or into the lives we lead.

Excess is often now the order of the day and advertising fuels that excess. A sobering question for all of us is: of all the things we spoil ourselves with, what do they really add to our lives? And this is a time for asking the question: is there an area of our lives where we need to be more moderate, where we need to be more temperate?

And we ask those questions not to accuse ourselves or run

ourselves down or to make life more difficult but in order to bring into our lives the kind of balance that will help us to live more human and ultimately more satisfying lives.

The question for each one of us on Temperance Sunday is: what is the area of my life that is creating an imbalance, that is putting my life out of focus? And each of us can answer that question for ourselves. For some people it will be simply saying: I need to control my consumption of alcohol, the way I drink is upsetting not just the balance of my own life but the lives of those most precious to me in the world. Anyone who has grown up in a family where there was a problem with alcohol wouldn't wish it on their worst enemy. So there may be questions for us there around that addiction or around another addiction.

There may be questions in other areas too, like work or rather the obsession we can sometimes have with work. At the end of life, married people who are workaholics invariably regret that they didn't spend more time with their families, that they missed out so much in life and in family due to their obsession with work and while a part of them always knew that, the rest of them didn't allow that question to be asked. So it was work and work and work or money and money and money or success and success and success or sometimes even greed and greed and greed for land or property or power or whatever. And gradually lives go out of shape, people lose the sense of balance, and all the things that they would say are important – spouse, family, children, home, health – all of them are sacrificed on the altar of work or money or success or whatever.

A useful question for all of us to ask is: what is the great obsession of my life and who's paying the price for it? For example you can find parents who are obsessed with perfection. Everything has to be right, everything has to be in its place. Every exam has to have honours attached to it. Life is about a series of boxes and everything has to be in its right box and everyone has to jump from one box to the next. And sometimes it can happen that when children don't live up to the perfection that some parents seem to expect and even demand, it can happen that on the altar of that expectation the relationship between parent and child can sometimes be sacrificed.

The same can happen between spouses. One spouse's obsession can bring to bear on the other spouse a demand that creates an imbalance and that makes it difficult to sustain a married relationship. And often it's only when the damage is done, that people can see clearly how the damage was done.

So in all of our lives the question we all need to ask ourselves is: where's the imbalance in my life now? where's the obsession that's taking a toll not just on my own life but on the lives of those around me? And what can I do to moderate that obsession? What can I do to begin to control it?

Part of the answer is recognising the area of our lives where we need to begin to say *No* to ourselves. And even though saying *No* isn't something that we understand very well nowadays, the beginning of Lent offers us an opportunity to do just that, an opportunity to try to bring an element of moderation into the area of our lives that is creating an imbalance.

So we can do it, if we recognise the problem and are motivated to seek a solution. That's what Lent is about. Seeing the problem and getting the motivation. So first why not give some thought to recognising the imbalance in your life. (And if you have trouble recognising it just ask your nearest and dearest and they'll be delighted with the opportunity to let you know.)

I know it's not easy. We're not used to it. We've got out of the hang of saying *No* to ourselves. We've forgotten how to put up with things. We're so comfortable that we don't know what we'd do if the electricity was off even for a day, if we hadn't X number of channels on the television, if we couldn't go to the pub X number of nights a week or if we hadn't the facilities that modern life offers us.

Before this we were more used to putting up with things. There was a language of self-denial and sacrifice that we knew how to speak but in more comfortable times we've forgotten the words.

So the challenge is to recognise whatever the imbalance is in our lives, to devise a strategy to moderate our excesses and to connect it to the season of Lent during which we prepare to celebrate the passion, death and resurrection of Jesus Christ.

A WEDDING DAY (1)
Intersection

NIALL Williams is an Irish writer. He's written two very successful novels. His first was called *Four Letters of Love* and his second is *As it is in Heaven*. They're love stories really but what makes them different is the sense of destiny or fate or providence – whatever you want to call it – that runs through them. It's almost as if the main characters are so destined to meet and fall in love, that everything that happens to them, everything they say and everything they do, is moving them inexorably towards a destination that, in a sense, is almost outside their control.

You know the way people say, that there was a destiny, a fate about their meeting and their marrying; a destiny that wouldn't and couldn't be denied; a sense that people looking back at life can sometimes see a pattern or a plan that moved them towards a particular decision or conclusion.

That's probably true in some sense because no matter how *we* try to organise life, life can end up organising *us*. No matter how we plan the future, much of life seems haphazard and unpredictable. No matter how we focus on what we *want,* life and nature and providence can often decide what we actually *get.*

On the day of a wedding, when the air is charged with happiness and joy and celebration and promise, there's a sense that a couple marks out a new life, a life that is very much of their own making. There's a sense that everything that's happening on a wedding day, is happening because the couple involved decided that it would happen.

And that, of course, is, in the main, true. We're all here by invitation. We wouldn't be here if Michelle and Ed weren't here.

We wouldn't be here unless there was a decision on their part to marry in this place and on this day. And we're here because of the definitive decisions they've made that have brought them to this day, to draw, what the politicians used to call, in happier times, 'a line in the sand.'

But even though all of that is true, even though this day and the happiness that, for them, please God will flow from it, even though all of that is of their making, the line they draw in the sand today is a line that they don't draw on their own.

Michelle and Ed arrive at this day, for better or for worse, carried along on the experiences and attitudes and values that have shaped their lives until this point in time. And they carry across that line in the sand, elements of life, of love, of hope, of faith that will continue to run through their relationship every day of their married life.

This present day is full of hope and promise for the future not just because of their love for each other, not just because of the thought and preparation that they have invested in this decision, not just because of the kind of people they are, but because where they are today and where they will be in the future has all to do with where they were in the past.

This day, important and all as it is, this day doesn't stand on its own; it looks into the future supported and bolstered by what has happened in the past. That's not to say that today is just a bridge of hope between the past and the future. No, today couldn't be more special, because this is one of those points in life that changes everything.

I remember the philosopher John O'Donohue once saying that at every moment of time there are people somewhere undergoing the kind of significant experience that will change forever their perspective in life from this moment on: a young person is killed in an accident; a relationship breaks down irretrievably; a baby is born; someone commits suicide. And as and from that precise day, that particular moment, everything is judged in terms of that monumental happening. Wasn't that the year before John died? Wasn't that the winter after the big row? Wasn't that the summer before Mary was diagnosed? And these monumental happenings carry such a weight of a lived life that they are indelibly imprinted on our consciousness.

A wedding day is one such monumental happening because it

too carries a great weight. A wedding day sings a song of love because we recognise the hopeless inadequacy of the human mind to understand the miracle of love. So we communicate it in symbol and in song. A wedding day is like writing a poem that puts flesh on important words like 'fidelity' and 'permanence.' A wedding day is about making a commitment at a time when the word 'commitment' has lost some of its popular flavour.

A wedding day is about holding the hand of the person you love most in the world and walking both humbly and confidently into whatever pattern the future holds. A wedding day is about saying, calmly and clearly before God and before those closest to us in the world, the most important words that two people can say to each other.

That's what all this is about. Ed and Michelle have chosen to say those words in this sacred space, this place that sings a silent hymn to the things that, in life and in death, mean most to us.

This place of worship, of prayer, of reflection, this place where Michelle made her First Confession, her First Communion, her Confirmation, this is the sacred space where she has invited Ed to exchange vows that will forever shape the life that they will lead from this point on.

For them, on this day, this is a place both of ending and of beginning. This present moment is an intersection between past and future, between hope and promise, between the dreams that have brought them to this day and what those dreams will be.

In the old days farmers had to flail the corn and then on a breezy day throw it into the air to separate the wheat from the chaff. In a comparative sense this is what Ed and Michelle will do in a moment as they exchange their vows. They are taking the grain and the chaff together and throwing it into God's air and before God's altar, so that the kernel of this day is left on the ground in front of us: the kernel of commitment, of fidelity and of permanence that they will bring with them from this day into the rest of their lives.

I now invite Ed and Michelle to exchange their marriage vows and I invite their parents, their families and their friends to witness to the sacrament of marriage which as members of God's family they will now confer on each other.

A WEDDING DAY (2)
The pilgrimage

I welcome you today to this church for the wedding Mass of John and Mary. This is a place steeped in history. It's a monument to the values and the traditions that have over the centuries given substance to the content and the practice of our Christian faith. For centuries there has been an unbroken tradition of Christian worship in this holy place; for centuries the Christian story has been told and retold; for centuries couples have been married; babies have been baptised; children have made First Communions and Confirmations; the dead have been buried from here; the joyful mysteries and the sorrowful mysteries of centuries of Christian life are written on the walls of this place.

So this parish church is a special place, a place that sings a silent hymn to the things that in life and in death mean most to us. This is a place where we come to worship our God, this is a place where we take time out, to pray, to reflect, to pick over the bits and pieces of our lives and to place in God's hands the hopes and the dreams and the worries and difficulties that are part and parcel of every life. In that sense (you could say) that this place is a place of pilgrimage. And today John and Mary have come to this special place, to this sacred spot to exchange their marriage vows, and their journey to this place is part and parcel of their own pilgrimage of life and of faith.

A pilgrimage isn't so much a journey to a special place as the great journey of life itself. Because from birth to death each of us travels the great journey of life. And from time to time along that road of life things happen to us and we make things happen to us that change our lives significantly. There are, as we all know, great parts of life, great chunks of that journey that we can't control. But we know too that there are parts of life that we can control, that we can change for better or for worse.

There are crossroads that we meet in life that are there whether we like it or not and there are crossroads that we shape for ourselves because of the choices we make in life.

Today John and Mary have created a crossroads for themselves, a crossroads that is very much of their own making. They were both brought up in different families, they grew up in different townlands and somewhere along the road of life their paths crossed. It could have been just another meeting between two people but from that point on, their lives and their future started to come together.

That happened because they decided it should happen and today they are making another decision that confirms their intention to travel forever along whatever road of life awaits them from this point in time.

In the years since they've met their love for each other has grown to such a degree that they have decided before families, before friends and before God, they have decided in this public and formal way to be married as a Christian couple.

And those of us who know them and those who love them are happy and privileged today to witness to their love and to witness too to the commitment they make together in Christian marriage not just today but for the rest of their lives.

John and Mary are today making a choice that will remain with them all their days. They're making that choice freely and they're making that choice in the full knowledge of what it means. They are aware today through their preparation for marriage, through the example of other couples, through the love they have seen in their own homes, they are aware of what Christian marriage involves. They're not just getting married today, they're getting married as Christians. People may marry in mosques or synagogues or wherever and all of them are married but we believe that the marriage of two baptised Christians is something different. So different in fact that we call it a sacrament, a sign of God's love and God's life in the sharing of the love of two people and the commitment that goes with it from this day on - a commitment to faithfulness and fidelity to one another, to the permanency of their marriage, to a shared life where that fidelity and that permanency will create an atmosphere of acceptance, of trust and of love that will help them to overcome the tensions and the failures that are part and parcel of every human relationship.

John and Mary know that Christian marriage is about sharing - a sharing that is complete and absolute, a sharing of hearts and bodies and minds, a sharing of time, of decisions, of material possessions, a sharing of ideas, of feelings, of attitudes, as complete a sharing as it is possible to have.

And they know too that Christian marriage is above all a sharing of love. It's a statement that the love that has brought you to this day will be made to grow and to deepen all the days of your lives. It's a commitment you make that from now on you will mingle your two lives into one together and forever you will live and love and grow together and forever, you will live a community of love open to the children that God may send you and to the community in which you live.

For John and Mary today is for them the end of one dream and the beginning of another. It's our prayer for them today that their dream will come true. And they can indeed confidently hope that it will. For just as Jesus set out in life with the advantage of his life in Nazareth behind him, so too John and Mary can look back in confidence and in gratitude over the pilgrimage of their lives to the preparations for this day.

Their parents in the short years of childhood and adolescence have taught them what love means, what respect is, what it means to live a Christian life, and out of the richness of their own Nazareths has come the love they share today.

Our prayer for them is that as they face the future together that their lives may be full of kindness, of understanding and of forgiveness. Life, as we all know, is full of ups and downs, good times and bad times, joys and sorrows. May the love that they share today and the support that God gives them in their married life help them to grow closer through the ups and downs of life. Here in this hallowed place, a place of permanence and of commitment and of faith, I now invite John and Mary to exchange their marriage vows and I invite their parents, their families and their friends to witness to the sacrament of marriage which as members of God's family they will now confer on each other.

165

DEATH IN SPRING
Daffodils

THERE is a still-point in every year when you suddenly
realise that Spring is here. You're walking along a road and
suddenly you see snowdrops under the trees. Or you walk along
a lane and suddenly there are yellow daffodils everywhere.

The other day when I was visiting Mary I noticed a bunch of
yellow daffodils on her front window. Daffodils, precursors of life
and growth and new beginnings. It was lovely to see them,
because daffodils are always full of hope and life and spring, and
yet there was a great sadness about them because we knew that
the reality of Mary's impending death somehow made them seem
out of season.

If Mary had lived a long life and if she had died at the
intersection, say, of autumn and winter, her death might seem to
have a certain symmetry to it.

But dying as she has at such a relatively young age and at the
turn of spring, her death seemed very much out of sync with the
season.

And even though we know, and Mary knew, that time and tide
and birth and death have their own seasons, even though she
and we could reasonably have expected her life to move through
several other spring-times, Mary knew and we know, if there's
nothing else we know, that life and death are ultimately in God's
hands.

And to try to make meaning of Mary's life and death, we have
to move in faith to another season of the year, to the Easter
experience. And we find ourselves at the heart of that confluence
of suffering and release, of expectation and hope, of leave taking
and home coming that marks the reality of this death for us.

For the last few years of her life, Mary was at the centre of that cross-roads between pain and ease, between suffering and release, between belonging and departing, between leave-taking and home-coming, between the knowledge of the seriousness of her illness and the hope that her life might somehow continue. And she had a long and gallant struggle holding grimly on to life but knowing too that her life and everything it meant, for her and those she loved and those who loved her, was gradually slipping away. But in the small hours when dark thoughts flit across the mind and the courage wavers, she remained close to her own, and she slipped quietly away, closing a chapter of her life and of the life of all those who loved her.

Death came for her, as death often eventually comes, quietly and without fuss. Her gentle and gracious spirit gave her a dignity and a presence that attested both to her deep faith and to her uncompromising love for John and for her family.

It's no exaggeration to say that apart from the love she experienced from those closest to her, Mary was deeply respected and, I think it can be said, deeply loved by those who were part of her extended parish family of neighbours and friends. But even though the memories are good and generous and loving – and that's a great consolation – that's not to say, in any sense, that her death is something that can be dealt with comfortably.

There is, as we know, a great difference, between an idea and the reality behind it. It's one thing to discuss something in theory, it's quite a different matter to work it out in practice. We could have conversations – as we often do – about the possibility of death, about the most obvious fact of life being the fact of death. We can discuss death even our own death with impunity but when that death comes, it's quite a different matter altogether.

When the hand of death is laid on the shoulder of someone close and important to us, death becomes not a natural and acceptable experience but a strange and sometimes frightening encounter with the unknown, a permanent and disquietening silence after a lifetime of movement and activity.

A person, a presence around us and (in a sense too) within us, is suddenly silent and those who remain are left to cope with the loss and the sadness that death always brings. At the same time coping with death, and dealing with grief is something that we don't do on our own. Of course the effort to cope with the death of someone close and important to us, that grieving we have to do on our own. But in that grief we are supported by the friendship and concern of other people and we are supported too by what our Christian faith tells us about death and what it means.

Because even though death means mystery and silence and finality – confronting mystery, listening to silence and accepting the finality of what it is – it also means seeing with the eyes of faith a reality that apart from faith we could hardly expect to make sense of. It means bringing to the front of our minds that perspective of resurrection, that belief in another life that is at very heart of the Christian experience.

And we can on this day bring that Easter perspective to what is happening now in this church. Because Mary had, in her own life, that Easter faith, that belief that when we die there is another reality beyond this life. This church was a place she attended to worship her God, to listen to his Word, to eat at his table and to try to situate the mystery of her own birth, life and death in the context of that faith.

So despite her early death, despite the sadness of her parting there are the good memories too, and the consolations that will help to ease her parting: the consolation of knowing that the stress and the pain of her illness are no more; the consolation of knowing that her spirit is now still and at peace; the consolation of her firm faith in a God who loved her in life and now welcomes her in death, that loving and welcoming and tolerant God who brought us into life, who blesses us with so much and so many, and who some day, not of anyone's making, who some day calls us through the door of death into a new and different and fuller life with him.

Even though I know that for those close to Mary, these days and the days to come will seem dark with longing for her presence and with loneliness in her absence. These days of spring and daffodils and new growth will be out sync with this season of their grieving but even though her life on this earth is over, her love and her presence will remain with them to encourage and strengthen them in the days and weeks and months ahead. May her gentle spirit rest in God's peace and may a forest of daffodils brighten her road and bring her safely home to God.

DEATH OF AN ELDERLY PERSON (1)
Unravelling the mystery

FOR much of the time, most of us tend to live life at a shallow enough level. Much of life, even the most important parts of life can be repetitive, even dull and we tend to move from day to day taking things for granted, presuming that life as we know it will continue along its predictable way.

Often we haven't time to think our way along. We haven't the luxury of the kind of space we need to live a reflective life and then suddenly the children have moved away from home or a spouse is dead or a life-long friend is no longer there and we find ourselves instinctively lapsing into reflection, looking at life as if it were a giant jig-saw that we simply can't fit together.

Margaret, the woman we mourn today, was a very reflective person. She had an active and instinctive intelligence. She read and pondered and reflected on the twists and turns of her life.

Earlier this year, Margaret celebrated her ninetieth birthday by coming to Mass in this church as she had so regularly done for so many years and she died last Thursday in her ninety-first year retaining to the end in the care of the North West Hospice in Sligo, retaining to the end a dignity and a poise and a bearing that were very much part of her life and of her own personal style . A life that had lasted almost the entire length of this century came quietly to a close like a ripened fruit dropping almost unnoticed from the tree of life. 'The Lord has given; the Lord has taken away. Praised be the name of the Lord.'

And what made Margaret's life complete wasn't just the happiness of her last years, or the fact that she had lived for more than ninety years on this earth, or the fact that a difficult illness could have devastated that bearing and poise she had.

What really brought a sense of completion to her life was her sense that her time had come, that her life had come full circle, that it was time to leave the stage with dignity and without regret.

She told me herself that she was happy to die, whenever God called her. She was ready and you felt not just that she was ready to go but that somehow she wanted to die, that there was business beyond that she wanted to attend to. And all of that was placed in the context of an unnervingly solid faith in a God who loved and cared for her.

Margaret was a woman of deep faith who lived a long and a decent life, and who brought hope and light into the world of those who knew her. And her God was a God who was part of the very texture of her life, a God who understood the dark moments of pain and suffering and a God who understood the happy and bright days of hope and promise, a God who knew her and whom she knew, a God of the everyday and the ordinary, a God who loved her in life and who now welcomes her in death.

So we mark her life and we welcome her death with acceptance and with joy. I know there is sadness too for those who knew her and loved her and that's part of the geography of death. The death of those we love is an experience that marks us for life. Not just because it's devastating at a personal level but also because in a more general sense in a world that has an answer almost to every question, there's a disconcerting silence about death.

Death disturbs us. Death sets us at odds with ourselves. It disturbs the easy pattern of our lives. It disrupts the usual parameters within which our existence in this world is shaped. It sets aside the boundaries that reassure us and we are left floundering in the great mystery of it all.

There's loss and regret and sadness. There's the experience of being at odds with ourselves. And there are questions that jump out at us in every waking hour, questions that lie in wait for us and that tumble out of our minds at the most unexpected moment.

There's a sense too that if we could we would write a different script for someone's life and death, we would want to write a different script for our own grieving. But that's outside and beyond what's within our power to make happen.

We sometimes think that the Christian religion should somehow surface the answers, should be able to make sense of it all. And it can't of course. All it can do is offer us broad strokes. All it can do is fill in parts of the background. All it can do is help us face the pain by providing us with rituals, at once painful and consoling.

But if we have a firm faith in a God of mercy and love, if we can situate our grieving in the presence of a God who loves us and cares us beyond all telling, then we can find a comfort and a consolation even in the most distressing of circumstances.

For Margaret, of course, and for all our loved ones, there are no more questions, no more imponderables, no more mystery. The bits of the jig-saw suddenly begin to fit. The questions unravel, the mystery disappears. 'The Lord has given; the Lord has taken away. Praised be the name of the Lord.'

Christ has died! Christ is risen! Christ will come again!

DEATH OF AN ELDERLY PERSON (2)
Now and at the hour of our death

E VERY Sunday we attend Mass we profess our faith in the
resurrection. Every Sunday in the Creed we say the words,
'. . . we look for the resurrection of the dead and the life of
would to come'. Thousands and for some probably millions of
times during a lifetime we say the Hail Mary and we end with
the words 'Pray for sinners, now and at the hour of our death.'
And often we say the Creed and pray the Hail Mary with little
thought of what the words mean.

'Holy Mary, Mother of God' we say over and over again, 'pray
for us sinners now and at the hour of our death. Amen.'

Annie, whom we mourn today, said the Hail Mary, thousands
indeed possibility millions of times. The Rosary was a staple part
of her spiritual diet.

The incantation and the repetition that is part and parcel of
the Rosary had become over the years part and parcel of her life.
And when the time came for her to leave this earth, it was the
Rosary that she wanted to say, it was that familiar and
reassuring incantation and repetition that she wanted to
experience as God called her home.

She had reached that point in her life where the words she
had repeated over a long time, 'Pray for us sinners now and at
the hour of our death. Amen,' where the words brought her life
to a close. And where the words, 'Now and at the hour of our
death' coalesced for her and God called her home.

Today we pay our final respects to Annie, a quiet and utterly
unassuming person, a gentle soul who lived in this place for
about fifty years.

I didn't know Annie that well but I'm told that she was a good neighbour, that she was of a very generous disposition and that she loved to sing. One thing I do know about her is that her religion was very special to her. Her faith was an important part of her life. And during the years that she lived in this place, she came very often to this sacred spot. This, for her, was a special place. So it's appropriate and fitting that her remains should be brought to this church for the rituals of death and burial.

The woman who knelt in those seats, the woman who knelt so often in her own kitchen to say the family Rosary, the woman for whom God was in the bits and pieces of every day is now, we can confidently say, close to the God who gave her life and the God who has taken that life back from her. That was her faith and that's our faith too. That's what has brought us not just to pay our respects to her today but to pray for the happy repose of her soul.

And that's what she would have wanted. The words she spoke in the Creed about death and resurrection today take on a special meaning for her. During the pilgrimage that life is for all people those of us who believe in the death and resurrection of our Lord and Saviour Jesus Christ look forward to a distant day when the pains and struggles of life will be no more, when the great mysteries of life and death will be resolved.

For Annie that has now happened. The door of death has opened and closed as she always believed it would and those words about death and resurrection that she repeated over and over again during the course of a long life, those words now have a fuller and more complete meaning.

And we can be confident that this day Annie is with God because the faith she had, the life she lived, the death she has gone through were all born out of a conviction and a belief that beyond that door of death, the God who gave her life and the God who would take that life from her, that that God was waiting to welcome her to a happiness that she had prepared for all her days.

And Annie could confidently go through the door of death, both because of her belief in the resurrection and also because the life she lived pointed her in the direction of unity with God and unity too with her husband John, who no doubt was there to welcome her home.

I mentioned earlier that Annie liked to sing. She had a lovely voice, I believe, and there's a sense in which, I think, people who have music of life in them can often touch something that is beyond the rest of us. There is often in musicians and in singers a deeper sense of the great mystery of it all, an ability almost to communicate at a level that others can't easily reach. They have, I believe, a keener sense of the language of celebration and suffering, of beginning and ending, of saying Hello and saying Goodbye.

Annie's song has now been sung, her life has come full circle, and today we offer that life to the God who gave her song and the God who could hear the song of her heart.

So we commend the soul of Annie to the God who loved her in life and now welcomes her in death. May the the angels lead her into paradise and may the martyrs come to welcome her and take her to the new and eternal Jerusalem. And may her gentle soul rest contently today in the peace and happiness of God's kingdom.

Leave-taking and home-coming

THERE is always a great sadness about death. No matter the time or place or season, death doesn't fit. Death, despite its inevitability and its universality, seems somehow out of touch with life, at odds with living.

Death has, you could say, a life of its own. Death comes in its own time, death comes in its own way. And death is like a clearance in the forest where we can distinguish the wood from the trees, what's important from what doesn't really matter all that much.

A few days ago it was clear that Martin had come to the end of his life. A serious illness five years ago marked time for him and he and Beatrice and their family were grateful for the extra years that God gave him. But his time had come. He had lived the eighty-three years God gave him with a life and a vigour that surely God intended. He had his work done, his prayers said. As Pope John XXIII used to say about himself, he had his bags packed. And even though he clung to life with grit and determination in the last days God gave him, his final illness and the discomforts it brought, eventually wore him out of life.

And that life had such a ripeness and a truth about it that death came softly and gently like a ripe fruit falling from the tree of life. But what particularly makes Martin's death such a natural conclusion to his life, was that the faith-life he lived for eighty-three years was lived as one long preparation for death. He lived a long time. He learned the lessons that only time and experience can teach. He carved his own wisdom out of a life lived in this place and above all he had a deep religious faith that informed his view of the way things fitted together.

A deep and rich .... his life, He
believed in the goodness and love of God; he recognised his own
failures and his own sinfulness; he knew that the life he had was
blessed by God in Beatrice, in his family, in his work, and in his
place. And it meant that the life he had would one day end and
re-begin in another form, in another life, by virtue of his faith in
the resurrection.

And that faith was as real to him as the sun that rose every
morning. God was as present to his life as the air that he
breathed every day. In simple terms he was a man who said his
prayers, a man for whom Mass wasn't a burden but a privilege, a
man for whom praying the Rosary – as he did so regularly –
wasn't an optional extra but a natural part of every day. When I
attended him in his final illness, it was clear how much he
appreciated receiving the Eucharist, how natural and instinctive
was his faith and how eager he was to be close to God as death
drew nearer.

I often think in ministering to people of Martin's generation,
the privilege it is to witness at first hand, the depth of faith that
his generation clung to in difficult times - to feel the sense of God
that's part and parcel of the very texture of their lives, to know
the consolations and the comforts that they glean from the
presence of God around them.

But we know too that though Martin's faith is and will be – in
the months and years ahead – a great comfort and consolation to
his wife and family, we know too that their experience now is
inevitably one of great sadness, sadness at parting with someone
so obviously and so deeply loved.

It's difficult to part with someone who's precious to us in life,
particularly someone who formed our lives by the way they lived
theirs, someone who influenced thoughts, words and actions in
ways that it takes a lifetime to explore. When we lose someone
we love, part of ourselves seems to die with them.

There are fragments of the lives and experience of our loved
ones that will for years to come awaken memories for us of the
people they were, the things they said, the ways they had:
fragments of times gone by that will forever keep the memory
alive, words spoken and events remembered that will flood into
the mind and continue to remind us of the person who's gone.

Martin's family will have their own fragments of his life that will help to keep his memory: Martin saying the Rosary, welcoming his grandchildren, going to a football match, sitting in his own chair and the one-thousand-and-one ordinary things that didn't seem to matter all that much but that will in future frame the memories of the husband, father, grandfather, brother, relative, neighbour and friend that he was.

For Beatrice and her family know in a way the rest of us can never know the life he lived, the contribution he made to their lives and to their happiness and now the gap in their lives that will remain forever unfilled. For them there are, this morning, memories that are private and personal, fragments that for them will frame memories for them of the person Martin was, the life he lived, the death he has gone through.

It's not easy to say goodbye to someone we love because when a loved one dies part of life dies with them. At the same time it is easier to cope with the reality of death, when the person who has died had a lively faith in the goodness and mercy of God.

So I would say to Beatrice and to her family that it is right that they should mourn a loving husband and a loving father and a loving grandfather and it is right too that there should be sadness at the pain of parting. But I would say as well that this day is not just a leave-taking but also in a real sense a home-coming. There is too today a sense that Martin's life has run its course, so there will be too a comfort and a contentment in the weeks and years ahead that comes from recognising and accepting that God had called him home. And there will too in time be something of an Easter joy, based not on what we feel now but on Martin's faith in the resurrection of his Lord and Saviour Jesus Christ. Because at the end of the day that's what really matters. A life has been lived in the shadow of God's presence, the Word of God has been heard, the ways of God have been lived.

So today while there is the sadness and the sorrow of parting, while the sense of loss is real and tangible, there is a sense too that at another level our faith and Martin's faith in the resurrection of Jesus Christ gives substance to hope and have within them the promise of acceptance and eventually joy - even within the context of sadness and loss. The sadness of this death cannot take from the joy of God coming into our world because this death links us into another joy, the joy of an Easter morning.

177

DEATH OF A MOTHER
Safely home

AS I drove to my native Ballycastle on the North coast of Mayo for my mother's funeral Mass, a great black cloud over Moyne suddenly became the backdrop for a spectacular rainbow. Every one of the colours could be seen: violet, indigo, blue, green, yellow, orange and red. Each colour independently claiming its own space.

A poem of John O'Donoghue's came into my mind. It's called 'Beannacht' (Blessing) and John wrote it for his mother and, for many years, it was my prayer for my own mother. At home in Ballycastle she had lived on her own since my father's death nineteen years ago and we worried about her in case anything might happen to her. And this poem/prayer was for me a great consolation:

On the day / when the weight deadens / on your shoulders and you stumble, / may the clay dance / to balance you. And when your eyes / freeze behind / the grey window and the ghost of loss / gets in to you, / may a flock of colours, indigo, red, green / and azure blue / come to awaken in you a meadow of delight. / When the canvas frays / in the currach of thought / and a stain of ocean blackens beneath you, / may there come across the waters a path of yellow moonlight / to bring you safely home.

Safely home. On a grim and grey day the rainbow over Moyne and the colours in John O'Donoghue's poem provided an unexpected solace. They brought the bright promise of colour into a personal and family landscape of grief and loss. Light and colour after the darkness. Home after the journey. Resurrection after the death.

Mother had a slight heart attack on a Sunday morning and was taken to hospital. We worried her into what we imagined was an improvement and we settled her into sleep on the following Thursday night. Happy that she was contented we left her in caring hands for the night. Two hours later she was dead. Another heart attack had eased her into death, quietly and without fuss. We had celebrated her eighty-fifth birthday last September.

Seamus Heaney wrote somewhere

. . . we all knew one thing by being there. / The space we stood around / had been emptied / Into us to keep . . .

and anyone who is catapulted into that sharp and sensitive world of personal loss and the excruciating pain that attends it will know what Heaney means. Every family member encountered, every tear shed, every hand held or shaken, every comforting hug, every face that offered even a glimpse of understanding, every ebb and flow of the great river of sympathy and condolence we were privileged to experience are all stored away in a precious memory-bank. Every moment of her final days, every iota of distraction and unease during her removal, funeral Mass and burial are now part of a series of tapes that we will play over and over again in our minds for as long as we have breath in our bodies. The loss of her presence, the sense of gratitude to God for the gift of her life, the consolations that we convince ourselves we feel are all part of an experience etched forever on our consciousness. *The space we stood around had been emptied / Into us to keep.*

Mother had nine children, six sons and three daughters, among them triplets (two girls and a boy) who died just after they were born. She rarely mentioned her dead children - at least not to us - but she grieved them for more than half a century. She gave birth to them in Castlebar Hospital and every time she returned there as a patient, she relived that difficult time. In the dreary Forties there was no counselling, little sympathy, no perception of how devastating the grieving of a child, let alone three children, could be. In the wisdom of the day, Mother - like so many others - was expected to pull herself together. It seems in retrospect an unnecessarily cruel and diminishing time, something that I find myself wanting to rail against in these sharply-sensitive days.

But mostly what I feel about Mother - apart from a great sadness and a terrible loss mediated through an unsurprising love - is an overwhelming sense of gratitude. She was good to us beyond words. She worked and worried, sewed and knitted, baked and cooked. Fair Isle jumpers, Báinín sweaters, crocheted garments, complicated curtains, embroidered dance-costumes. And God was good to us in leaving her for more than sixty years as the heart of our home in Ballycastle.

I find her now, in these precious but difficult days, slipping in and out of my thoughts as if she hasn't left us.

I find her presence in my sentimental journeys through the places of my childhood.

I find her in a colourful phrase someone uses or a John McCormack song on the radio or in the sight of a neighbour who was part of the wider family of care that surrounded her in her declining years.

I find her in Seamus Heaney's sonnet sequence *Clearances* (in *The Haw Lantern)*, beautifully crafted epiphanies of love and transcendence, written for his own mother and conjuring up those enduringly precious childhood moments where, for example, *sheets she'd sewn from ripped-out flour sacks* were stretched and folded:
The fabric like a sail in a cross-wind, / They made a dried-out undulating thwack, / So we'd stretch and fold and end up hand in hand...

I find her in the side chapel of St Bridget's Church in Ballycastle where she prayed so often and in the places in Ballina which she shopped (and occasionally complained) for so many years.

And I find her too, discomforting and heart-rending as it is, in the contorted face of an old woman in a hospital bed as personal dignity and independence are sacrificed to disorientation, illness and old age.

A whole lifetime of knowing and loving her is not preparation enough for leaving her no matter how I rationalise it. But that is not of my doing. The longer I live the less I seem to know about the things that really matter. All I think I do know is that the tapestry of life, folded or unfolding like the white sheet just off the line, is full of bitter-sweet moments that need to be unambiguously cherished. In the words of poet Pádraig J. Daly

I feel no anger at your death, / Flailing and floundering though I am / In loss; / More, / An upsurge of gratitude / For the way you blessed us: / We have known the bounty of Autumn / And settle into Winter / With / harvest of rich apples.

May the colours of the rainbow continue to brighten the darkness of all who grieve for my mother, Ellen Hoban, and may there come across the waters a path of yellow moonlight to bring her safely home.